The Random Book of…

DAVID

Dave Blake

The Random Book of...

DAVID

Well, I didn't know that!

All statistics, facts and figures are correct as of March 31st 2009.

Published By:

Stripe Publishing Ltd
First Floor, 3 St. Georges Place, Brighton, BN1 4GA

Email: info@stripepublishing.co.uk
Web: www.stripepublishing.co.uk

First published 2009

A catalogue record for this book is available from the British Library.

10-digit ISBN: 1-907158-03-0
13-digit ISBN: 978-1-907158-03-2

Printed and bound by Gutenberg Press Ltd., Malta.

Editor: Dan Tester
Illustrations: Jonathan Pugh (www.pughcartoons.co.uk)
Typesetting: Andrew Searle
Cover: Andy Heath

INTRODUCTION

"There's an awful temptation to just keep on researching. There comes a point where you just have to stop, and start writing"
Pulitzer prize-winning biographer **David McCullough** (b. 1933)

Oh, yes. So many 'Davids'… so little time…

This book doesn't aim to be the definitive book on 'David'. Its aim is more a snapshot of 'Davids' through history. The good, the bad, the pioneering, the inventive, the funny and the psychotic – you'll find a good selection of your favourites in here.

The chances are, however, you'll find quite a few missing. That doesn't mean that those absent 'Davids' were thought of any less. It's just that they weren't pulled out of the metaphorical hat.

The very nature of this book is in the title. Firstly, it's jam-packed full of 'Davids' and the name's derivatives (arguably containing more 'David' name-checks than any other book in printed history apart from the Hebrew Bible!), and, secondly, it is 'Random', which the dictionary defines as '… chosen without any definite plan, aim or pattern'.

So don't get grizzly about the glaring omissions, just settle back and dip into the wonderful world that is 'David'.

Dave Blake

WHERE DOES DAVID COME FROM?

David is a common English male name and surname
that derives from the Biblical Hebrew meaning 'beloved'.
Among the 'name days' celebrated are March 1st for St.
David of Wales and December 29th for King David, as well
as June 25th for St. David of Sweden.

Arguably the most prominent bearer of the name was
David – second king of Israel. The name occurs over one
thousand times in the Hebrew Bible, putting it third behind
Moses and Abraham.

A common derivation in Israel is Dudi. In Wales there
are variants such as Dafydd, Daveth, Dewi, Daf, which
commonly becomes Taf or Taffy, and also Dai – once a
name in its own right, meaning 'shining'. In Arabic culture
it becomes Daud or Dawood.

In Georgia it translates as Davit or Dato, and in Croatia
it becomes Davor. In Australia it is sometimes shortened
to Davo, and in South Africa to Dovi or Dov. Female
equivalent names include Davida or Davina. But the most
common diminutives are Davey, Davie, Davy or – easily the
most popular one – Dave.

MOST POPULAR BIRTH NAMES DAVE

2003

UK:
1st Jack
2nd Joshua
3rd Thomas
49th **David**

2004

UK:
1st Jack
2nd Joshua
3rd Thomas
56th **David**

2005

UK:
1st Jack
2nd Joshua
3rd Thomas
60th **David**

2006

UK:
1st Jack
2nd Thomas
3rd Joshua
66th **David**

2007

UK:
1st Jack
2nd Thomas
3rd Oliver
64th **David**

SOME CONTINENTAL FOOTBALLING DAVES WITH OVER 50 CAPS

David Carabott (Malta); 121 caps & 12 goals (1987-2005)
Edgar Davids (Holland); 74 caps & 6 goals (1994-2005)
David Trezeguet (France); 71 caps & 34 goals (1998-2008)
Davor Šuker (Croatia); 69 caps & 45 goals (1990-2002)
David Rozehnal (Cz. Rep.); 52 caps & 0 goals (2004-2009*)
David Albelda (Spain); 51 caps & 0 goals (2001-2009*)

(* still playing)

VOLCANIC DAVID

On the morning of May 18th 1980, American volcanologist
David Johnston (1949-1980) was manning an observation
post about five miles from the volcano Mount St. Helens
in Washington State. Although the U.S. Geological
Survey had predicted a conventional vertical eruption, the
mountain's first for 123 years, Johnston believed it would
explode laterally. Unfortunately for him, he was right. As
the mountain erupted, its north face collapsed and Johnston
was killed by a torrent of rock, steam and gasses.

"Vancouver! Vancouver! This is it!"
David Johnston's last words on his radio transmitter.

———◆———

LOCAL RADIO DAVE

In 2005 'Project Bullseye' created two of the most
influential names in BBC local radio. **Dave and Sue** were
fictional radio listeners created to facilitate audience growth.
Dave was a self-employed plumber and Sue a school
secretary. Both were described as 55-year-old divorcees with
grown-up children.

They shopped at ASDA and wore casual clothes. Dislikes
included high culture and politics. They saw the world as a
dangerous and depressing place, and they hoped that radio
would be something that would cheer them up and make
them laugh. All BBC local radio presenters were given these

descriptions and required to deliver programmes that Dave and Sue would enjoy listening to.

"Morning all. Whatever job you do on station, make sure this week, you broadcast to DAVE AND SUE – people in their fifties. ONLY put on callers sounding in the 45-64 range... I don't want to hear really elderly voices... ONLY talk about things that are positive and appealing to people in this age range..."
Managing editor of BBC Radio Solent, Mia Costello, sends a memo to her staff.

⟫◆⟪

SOME COCKNEY RHYMING SLANG DAVIDS

Davey Crocket: Pocket
David Batty: Tatty
David Blaine: Insane
David Boon: Spoon
David Gower: Shower
David Hockney: Cockney
David Jason: Mason
David Mellor: Stella (beer)
David Starkey: Parky (cold)

POP DAVES

The Dave Clark Five would give The Beatles a run for their money, when both bands spearheaded the English pop 'invasion' of the USA. Led by drummer **Dave Clark** (b. 1939) they were promoted as the 'Tottenham Sound' in response to the 'Mersey Beat' phenomenon happening in Liverpool.

They had twelve Top 40 UK hits including Glad All Over, which knocked The Beatles from the number one spot in 1964. However, the pop-combo fared better in the States where they broke the Billboard chart Top 40 on no less than seventeen occasions.

Dave Harman (1943-2009) was a Swindon-based police cadet when he attended the scene of a fatal road accident. It turned out to be the crash that killed Eddie Cochran and badly injured Gene Vincent.

Harman eventually left the police and, with four friends, formed **Dave Dee, Dozy, Beaky, Mick & Tich**. Between 1965 and 1969, the group spent more weeks in the UK Singles chart than The Beatles with hits that included; The Legend of Xanadu and Bend It, the latter of which was used in 1981 by artists Gilbert & George as the soundtrack for a video.

A COUPLE OF BRITISH SOAP AWARD WINNING DAVIDS

David Neilson and Julie Hesmondhalgh as Roy and Hayley Cropper (Best On Screen Partnership) *Coronation Street* 2004

David Platt played by Jack P. Shepherd (Villain of the Year) *Coronation Street* 2008

GEEKY DAVID

David J. Bradley (b. 1949) worked on the original IBM PC and invented the Control-Alt-Delete key combination used to reboot computers.

"I may have invented it, but Bill (Gates) really made it famous."
David J. Bradley

SENSITIVE HUNK DAVID

David Hasselhoff (b. 1952) has portrayed two of the most iconic characters in TV history; Michael Knight in the fantasy action series *Knight Rider*, where he co-starred alongside a talking car, and as chief lifeguard Mitch Buchannon in *Baywatch*.

But he is also a hugely successful recording star. In Germany, following the end of the Cold War, he was awarded 'Most Popular and Best Selling Artist of the Year' in 1989 for his aptly titled album Looking For Freedom, and was consequently invited to perform at the fallen Berlin Wall on New Year's Eve of that year. The title track became an anthem of the Berlin people and stayed at the top of the charts for two months.

"I find it a bit sad that there is no photo of me hanging on the walls in the Berlin Museum at Checkpoint Charlie."
David Hasselhoff on his lack of recognition for ending the Cold War!

KNEES UP DAVE

Dave Peacock (b. 1945) is the bass guitarist, and one half of pub singalong duo **Chas & Dave**. Along with Chas Hodges, they cornered the market in working-class, humorous London pub culture with classics such as Rabbit and Gertcha. Other hits included Snooker Loopy and Tottenham Hotspur's 1981 FA Cup Final song, Ossie's Dream. In the same year, however, they had to turn down the chance to record the theme song for *Only Fools and Horses* as they were in Australia.

Snooker loopy nuts are we
Me and him and them and me
We'll show you what we can do
With a load of balls and a snooker cue
Chas & Dave

SOME MORE POP & ROCK DAVIDS

David Crosby (b. 1941): Guitarist, singer and songwriter with The Byrds and Crosby, Stills, Nash & Young
David Knopfler (b. 1952): Founding member and rhythm guitarist of Dire Straits. He left during the recording of their third album. He is Mark Knopfler's younger brother
David Gates (b. 1940): American singer-songwriter with Bread
David A. Stewart (b. 1952): Musician and producer, best known for his work with The Tourists and The Eurythmics
David 'Shuffle' Steele (b. 1960): Bass guitarist with The Beat and Fine Young Cannibals
Dave Evans (b. 1953): Australian lead singer and, in 1973, co-founder of AC/DC. Bon Scott replaced him a year later
David Johansen (b. 1950): Lead singer and songwriter of the seminal punk band The New York Dolls
David Sylvian (b. 1958): Lead singer and songwriter for 'art rockers' Japan
David Gray (b. 1968): Singer/songwriter who had his first British number one album with *White Ladder* in 1998
David Coverdale (b. 1951): Lead vocalist with Deep Purple, and then Whitesnake
Dave Gilmour (b.1946): Pink Floyd guitarist and vocalist
Dave Vanian (b. 1956): Lead singer with The Damned
Dave Barker (b. 1948): One half of duo **Dave and Ansell Collins** who had a 1971 number one hit in the UK with Double Barrel.

NUCLEAR DAVID

At the beginning of the 1940s, American quantum physicist **David Bohm** (1917-1992) was studying for his doctorate under Robert Oppenheimer. Recognising his undoubted talent, Oppenheimer invited Bohm to work alongside him on the Manhattan Project – the production of the first atomic bomb.

But Bohm's potential appointment was blocked when it was discovered that he had previously been active in organisations such as the Young Communist League and the Committee for Peace Mobilization. In 1943 he completed his Ph.D.

However, it was discovered, ironically, that some of his findings were deemed useful to the Manhattan Project, and as a result his findings were 'classified' – thus denying him access to his own work. It was Oppenheimer himself who persuaded the University of California to grant the Ph.D., and it came as little surprise when in 1949, at the beginning of the McCarthy communist 'witch hunts', Bohm was called upon to testify before the House Un-American Activities Committee. He was arrested and later acquitted having pleaded the Fifth Amendment and refused to give evidence against his colleagues. Bohm spent his final years in London where he became a Fellow of the Royal Society.

"The ability to perceive or think differently is more important than the knowledge gained."
David Bohm

INNOCENT TV DAVID

In the 1960s TV audiences on both sides of the Atlantic were glued to their sets in the hope that Dr. Richard Kimble, wrongly convicted of murdering his wife, would finally track down the real culprit and prove his innocence. It was **David Janssen** (1931-1980) who brought the doctor to life in over one hundred episodes.

A popular, hard-working, hard playing performer, Janssen also appeared as Harry in the detective series *Harry O* as well as racking up numerous leading film appearances including *The Green Berets* starring John Wayne. A heavy smoker who liked a drink, Janssen was just 48 when he died. According to a biography of Steven Spielberg, the lead role in his 1971 debut feature, *Duel*, was initially offered to Janssen before going to Dennis Weaver.

FICTIONAL HUNTED DAVID

David Mann, (Dennis Weaver), was the name of the motorist stalked by a seemingly demonic tanker truck in the 1971 Stephen Spielberg debut feature film *Duel*.

CHARMING STIFF-UPPER-LIP DAVID

Perhaps the most 'English' of English actors, London-born **David Niven** (1910-1983) claimed to have been born in Scotland as, to him, it sounded more romantic. He was just four years old when his father was killed during the Gallipoli Campaign of 1915. But following military training at Sandhurst, he became a Lieutenant Colonel and, during World War II, Niven's batman was one Private Peter Ustinov, who would later star alongside him in *Death on the Nile*. Niven fitted easily into the 'Hollywood Raj', a select group of British actors including Boris Karloff and Stan Laurel, who made their homes in Hollywood. Films included *Wuthering Heights* and *A Matter of Life and Death*. He was also Ian Fleming's original choice to play James Bond but was deemed too old for the part. However, he did get to play him in the 1967 spoof movie *Casino Royale*.

"I see my purpose in life as making the world a happier place to be in."
David Niven

ICONIC SWINGING SIXTIES DAVIDS

Along with fellow London East End photographer
Terence Donovan, **David Bailey** (b. 1938) captured
and often helped to create the celebrities, the spirit, the
culture and the fashionable chic of 'Swinging' London.
They photographed and socialised with models, actors,
musicians, gangsters and royalty and, in turn, became
celebrities themselves. In 1966 Italian film director
Michelangelo Antonioni made *Blow-Up*, a movie about a
fashion photographer whose camera captures a murder-in-
progress. The character of the snapper, played by **David
Hemmings**, was largely based on Bailey.

*"I never cared for fashion much, amusing little seams and witty little
pleats: it was the girls I liked."*
David Bailey

David Hemmings (1941-2003) became one of the
defining faces of the 1960s with appearances in *Blowup* and
Barbarella. He was also considered for the lead role of Alex
in the 1971 film of Anthony Burgess's controversial novel
A Clockwork Orange, but the part eventually went to Malcolm
McDowell. In the 1970s he turned his hand to directing and
was responsible for *Just a Gigolo* (1978) starring **David Bowie**
and Marlene Dietrich. In the 1980s he directed episodes of
popular U.S. TV series including *Airwolf* and *The A-Team*.

*"People thought I was dead. But I wasn't. I was just directing The
A-Team."*
David Hemmings

BROADWAY DAVID

In 1961, larger than life producer **David Merrick** (1911-2000) was behind a musical, *Subways Are For Sleeping,* which the New York critics had panned. But with the help of the city's telephone directory, he found seven New Yorkers with the identical names of the seven leading theatre critics, and invited them to the show. Merrick then garnered quotes off each of them including: "One of the few great musical comedies of the last thirty years" and "A fabulous musical. I love it", and used them for advertising. As a consequence, the show went on to run for nearly six months more.

"It is not enough that I should succeed – others should fail."
David Merrick

WISDEN 'CRICKETER OF THE YEAR' DAVIDS

David 'Lucky' Denton 1906
David Sheppard 1953
David Green 1969
David Bairstow 1976
David Gower 1979
David Hughes 1988
David Boon 1994

1960s HEARTTHROB DAVIDS

Manchester-born **Davy Jones** (b. 1945) was lead singer with the made-for-TV boy band The Monkees. Because of his size, his father had hoped he would become a jockey, but Davy had other ideas. Having appeared in *Coronation Street*, he became the Artful Dodger in the musical *Oliver!* While in New York he appeared on the *Ed Sullivan Show* in the same episode as The Beatles, who were making their first US appearance. *The Monkees* phenomena lasted five years and as a result of its popularity, another artist called David Jones had to change his name.

This particular namesake became **David Bowie**.

Jones also left his mark on *Star Trek* when the producers cast look-a-like Walter Koenig as Chekov in an attempt to attract a young female audience.

Glasgow-born **David McCallum** (b. 1933) became a sex symbol playing Russian secret agent Illya Kuryakin in *The Man from U.N.C.L.E.* Prior to this he had already made his mark in a number of classic British movies including *Hell Drivers* and *A Night to Remember*. However, during filming of the 1963 classic *The Great Escape*, co-star Charles Bronson jokingly told McCallum that he was going to steal his wife, Jill Ireland, away from him.

A few years later Ireland and Bronson married. McCallum would later repeat his role as a prisoner-of-war in the TV series *Colditz* as well as starring opposite Joanna Lumley in the sci-fi thriller series *Sapphire & Steel*.

CLASSICAL DAVID

David McCallum, Sr. (1897-1972), the father of 1960s pin-up David McCallum, was also the concertmaster violinist of the Royal Philharmonic Orchestra, the London Philharmonic Orchestra and the Scottish National Orchestra. It is alleged that McCallum was the inspiration for Led Zeppelin guitarist Jimmy Page to play his guitar with a violin bow.

⟫◆⟪

U.S. FILM DAVIDS

As a 15-year-old future director, screenwriter and producer **David Lynch** (b.1946) served as an usher at the Presidential Inauguration of John F. Kennedy. A decade later he began on a five-year journey to make his darkly surreal debut movie *Eraserhead*.

It became an instant cult classic and led to an offer from Mel Brooks, in his role as a producer, to make the 1980 film *The Elephant Man*. Other critically acclaimed projects would follow including *Blue Velvet* (1986), *Wild at Heart* (1990), *Mulholland Drive* (2001) as well as the TV series *Twin Peaks* – on which he collaborated with Mark Frost.

George Lucas offered him the 1983 blockbuster *Star Wars VI – Return of the Jedi*, but Lynch turned it down in the belief it would be more Lucas's vision rather than his own. Instead he went off and made his own poorly received blockbuster *Dune*.

Another who was offered the job of directing *Star Wars VI – Return of the Jedi*, but declined, was Canadian-born **David Cronenberg** (b. 1943). For over thirty years he has been one of the leading exponents of the horror film genre, where his movies often explore people's fear of infection and transformation. A formidable list of credits include *Shivers, Rabid, The Brood, Scanners, Videodrome, The Dead Zone, The Fly, Naked Lunch, Crash*, and, in a departure from his usual style, *M. Butterfly*.

"We've all got the disease – the disease of being finite. Death is the basis of all horror."
David Cronenberg

Director **David Fincher** (b. 1962) first caught the attention of producers in his early twenties after directing a commercial for the American Cancer Society in which a foetus was depicted smoking a cigarette. Having made the disappointingly received *Alien 3*, he went on to begin a long-term collaboration with Brad Pitt with the film *Se7en* (1995). They would work together again on *Fight Club* (1999), and *The Curious Case of Benjamin Button* (2008).

"You have a responsibility for the way you make the audience feel, and I want them to feel uncomfortable."
David Fincher

For the last thirty-odd years American filmmaker **David Zucker** (b. 1947) – along with brother Jerry and frequent collaborators Jim Abrahams, Pat Proft and Craig Mazin

– have specialised in parodying various film genres. As producer, writer or director, Zucker's output has included such classics as *Airplane!*, *Police Squad!*, *Naked Gun* and the *Scary Movie* series.

Some IG Nobel Prize Winning Davids

These parody-Nobel Prize awards are given each year for ten achievements that first make people laugh, and then make them think. Practically all the following awards were shared with individuals or groups not called 'David'.

David Jacobs 1993 (Psychology)
For concluding that people who believe aliens from outer space kidnapped them probably were indeed kidnapped.

David B. Busch 1995 (Literature)
For the research report, *Rectal Foreign Bodies: Case Reports and a Comprehensive Review of the World's Literature*, the citations include one patient's remarkable collection consisting of spectacles, a suitcase key, a tobacco pouch and a magazine.

David Dunning 2000 (Psychology)
A report entitled, *Unskilled and Unaware of It: How Difficulties in Recognising One's Own Incompetence Lead to Inflated Self-Assessments*.

David Schmidt 2001 (Physics)
For his partial solution to the question of why shower curtains billow inwards.

David Stuart 2003 (Physics)
A report entitled *An Analysis of the Forces Required to Drag Sheep over Various Surfaces*.

David Gadian 2003 (Medicine)
For presenting evidence that the brains of London taxi

drivers are more highly developed than those of their fellow citizens.

David Sims 2008 (Literature)
His study *You Bastard: A Narrative Exploration of the Experience of Indignation within Organisations.*

⇒•◆•⇐

PHILOSOPHICAL DAVID

Controversial Scottish philosopher **David Hume** (1711-1776) rejected metaphysics in favour of the empirical approach; that human knowledge is born from observation and experience.

He held boldly sceptical views on a wide range of philosophical subjects, most notably religion, and argued that 'belief' should not be based on testimonies of alleged miraculous events, and therefore that these religions should be wholly rejected. These views ultimately prevented him from getting desired academic appointments. When biographer and diarist James Boswell visited him shortly before his death, Hume is alleged to have stated that the possibility of life after death was a 'most unreasonable fancy'.

"Generally speaking, the errors in religion are dangerous; those in philosophy only ridiculous"
David Hume

Country David

Comedy banjo player **David 'Stringbean' Akeman** (1915-1973) got his name after the judge at a talent contest forgot his name and introduced him to the crowd as "string beans".

Because he was tall and thin, the name stuck and in the 1950s he was one of the major stars at the Grand Ole Opry in Nashville, Tennessee. Never one to trust the banks with his money, it was well known that he kept considerable amounts of cash handy. In November 1973 he and his wife returned home after a performance and were shot dead by two would-be burglars.

⬥

Irish Comedy Dave

Dublin-born comedian **Dave Allen** (1936-2005) became a Butlins Redcoat at Skegness, and, in 1959, made his first TV appearance on the popular talent show *New Faces*. But it wasn't until 1967 that he got his own series, *Tonight with Dave Allen*.

This was followed by a transfer from ITV to the BBC, and would culminate in the hugely successful *Dave Allen at Large*. His gag-style was relaxed and intimate – always seated on a stool with a cigarette and a whiskey. His subjects were mostly the irritating trivialities of life, and his targets were, more often than not, religious institutions. Allen was also notable for the lack of half his index finger, and spent his career telling differing stories as to how he lost it – one being that he cut it off to avoid National Service.

"Goodnight, God bless, and may your God go with you."
Dave Allen

━━◆◆◆━━

DAVID COPPERFIELD DAVIDS

American illusionist **David Copperfield** (b. 1956) has made the Statue of Liberty disappear, levitated over the Grand Canyon and walked through the Great Wall of China. But, he failed in the seemingly simpler task of opening a restaurant. His themed eatery called Magic Underground was to have computerised devices that interacted with the guests, and waiting staff who would perform magic tricks whilst delivering orders.

However, the project was eventually aborted. More recently Copperfield claims to have discovered the 'Fountain of Youth' in the Bahamas, which is currently being studied by biologists and geologists.

In 1849 Charles Dickens's novel ***David Copperfield*** was first published in nineteen monthly instalments, costing one shilling each. Its full title was *The Personal History, Adventures, Experience and Observation of David Copperfield the Younger of Blunderstone Rookery.* Those who have played the part in film or on TV include Robert Hardy, Ian McKellen, Daniel Radcliffe and, in an animated version, Julian Lennon.

In the early 1980s, Yorkshire-born **David Copperfield** starred alongside Tracey Ullman and Lenny Henry in the TV sketch show *Three of a Kind*. However, of the three, he failed to experience TV longevity.

FICTIONAL SAVING-THE-PLANET DAVID

David Levinson (Jeff Goldblum) was the cable TV engineer, chess enthusiast and environmentalist in the blockbuster movie *Independence Day* (1996) who hatched a plan to repel the alien invasion.

ENVIRONMENTAL DAVID

London-born botanist **David Bellamy** (b. 1933) became a regular face on TV during the 1970s and 80s. Series included *Bellamy's Backyard Safari*, for the BBC, and *Botanic Man* for ITV, as well as regular guest appearances on other shows.

Bellamy's fame reached new heights when he was regularly parodied by comedian Lenny Henry on the cult children's Saturday morning TV show *Tiswas*. Although still very much involved in environmental campaigns, he has caused controversy by standing for the anti-European Union Referendum Party in 1997, and stating his case for global-warming scepticism.

"Well gwapple me gwapenuts!"
Lenny Henry's Bellamy-parody catchphrase on Tiswas

UK Sitcom-Creating Davids

David Croft (b. 1922) has quite simply been responsible
for some of Britain's best-loved sitcoms. As writer, director
and producer Croft has had three major collaborators: first
Jimmy Perry with whom he created *Dad's Army*, *It Ain't Half
Hot Mum*, *Hi-de-Hi!* and *You Rang, M'Lord?*, then with Jeremy
Lloyd, a partnership which spawned *Are You Being Served?*,
'Allo 'Allo! and *Grace and Favour*, and finally with co-creator
of *Oh, Doctor Beeching!* – ex-British Rail employee Richard
Spendlove.

*"I've been accused many times of writing stereotypes and I'm happy to
say yes, I do"*
David Croft

David Nobbs (b.1935) wrote material for comedy greats
including Kenneth Williams, Frankie Howerd, Les Dawson
and The Two Ronnies. But, amongst a variety of other
sitcoms, it was for his 1970s creation Reginald Perrin that
he is best known. Adapted from his own novels, *The Fall and
Rise of Reginald Perrin* – the often bizarre and surreal story
of a middle-aged executive constantly on the verge of a
metaphysical crisis – starred Leonard Rossiter as well as
introducing catchphrases that would enter the UK's popular
culture.

"I didn't get where I am today by selling ice cream tasting of bookends, pumice stone and West Germany"
CJ – Reggie Perrin's boss in The Fall and Rise of Reginald Perrin

➤◆◄

NATIONAL TREASURE DAVID

David Jason (b. 1940) was born David White. One of twins, he took the stage name Jason from his brother who died in infancy. Beginning his TV career in 1964 in ITV's long-defunct soap *Crossroads*, he went on to star in the often-bizarre children's sketch show *Do Not Adjust Your Set* alongside future Monty Python stars Michael Palin, Eric Idle and Terry Jones.

Jason was considered for the role of Lance-Corporal Jones in *Dad's Army* before landing the co-starring role of Granville in *Open All Hours* alongside Ronnie Barker. He would again appear with Barker in *Porridge*, as the aged inmate Blanco. But it was in 1981 that he landed his most enduring comedy role – Derek 'Del-Boy' Trotter – in *Only Fools and Horses*, which ran until 2003.

Subsequent acclaimed roles have included Skullion in *Porterhouse Blue*, Pa Larkin in *The Darling Buds of May*, and Inspector Jack Frost in *A Touch of Frost*. A measure of his enduring popularity was seen when, in 2006, he was voted 'TV's Greatest Star' by viewers of ITV.

STATESIDE 1970s HEARTTHROB DAVID

David Soul (b. 1943) first came to prominence in the 1973 movie *Magnum Force* where he played a vigilante police officer opposite Clint Eastwood's 'Dirty Harry'.

But it was in 1975 that he and long-time buddy Paul Michael Glaser formed one of the most popular cop partnerships in TV history. *Starsky and Hutch* became icons, and while Soul was strutting his stuff as Detective Ken Hutchinson, he also turned his hand to singing, twice enjoying number one hits in the UK. Nearly thirty years later he triumphantly took the lead role in the controversial West End stage production of *Jerry Springer – The Opera*. Now a British citizen, he has championed many social causes and, in 1997, famously supported war correspondent and independent candidate Martin Bell in his successful campaign to oust Conservative 'sleaze' MP Neil Hamilton from his Tatton seat.

David Cassidy (b. 1950) became the stuff of teenage girls' dreams in the music-based sitcom *The Partridge Family*. In the series he played eldest son Keith Partridge and Shirley Jones who was, in real life, Cassidy's stepmother, played his on-screen mother.

Surprisingly, as a recording artist, he only ever managed two number one hits in the UK and none in the USA, but he did become one of the world's highest paid live entertainers. However, it was in 1974 at the White City Stadium in London that he made the decision to stop touring following a frenzied stampede that would result in the death of 14-year-old Bernadette Whelan. The blameless Cassidy kept a low profile as far as live performances were concerned for a number of years, though he continued recording, and had hits including I Write The Songs, prior to Barry Manilow taking the number as his signature tune.

SOME PULITZER PRIZE-WINNING DAVIDS

David J. Mays 1953
David Donald 1961
David Brion Davis 1967
David M. Potter 1977
David Mamet 1984
David J. Garrow 1987
David K. Shipler 1987
David Herbert Donald 1988
David Henry Hwang 1989
David McCullough 1993 & 2002

STATESIDE SITCOM DAVIDS

Canadian **Dave Madden** (b. 1931) is best remembered as Reuben Kincaid, the on-screen manager of *The Partridge Family*. He was also a regular on the 'hip' American variety show *Rowan & Martin's Laugh-In*.

"Why couldn't I take a nice safe job? Like milking cobras!"
Reuben Kincaid on managing The Partridge Family

For eight years, between 1964 and 1972, **David White** (1916-1990) played Larry Tate, the irascible boss of advertising executive Darrin Stephens, in the American sitcom *Bewitched*. His movie career included supporting roles in *Sweet Smell of Success* (1957), and Billy Wilders' classic, *The Apartment* (1960). Tragedy was to hit him, however.

In 1958 his wife, actress Mary Welch, died in childbirth, and thirty years later his son Jonathan was killed in the terrorist bombing of Pan Am Flight 103 over Lockerbie in Scotland. White never fully recovered from his loss and died two years later.

David Hyde Pierce (b. 1959) is best known for his portrayal of neurotic psychiatrist Dr. Niles Crane in *Frasier*, and was initially cast because of his striking resemblance to his on-screen brother Frasier Crane (Kelsey Grammer). Hyde Pierce and Grammer have also reprised their roles in an episode of *The Simpsons* entitled *Brother From Another Series*, in which Grammer played his regular role of Sideshow Bob, and Hyde Pierce voiced his brother Cecil.

David Crane, the son of Dr. Niles Crane and Daphne Moon in *Frasier* was born in the very final episode of the series. His character was named after *Frasier* co-creator **David Angell** (1946-2001) who, along with his wife, was killed when the plane they were travelling in crashed into the World Trade Center in New York on September 11th 2001.

⋙◆⋘

SMOKIN' DAVID

American actor **David McLean** (1922-1995) began smoking at the age of 12 and went on to appear as 'The Marlboro Man', a rugged smoking cowboy, in numerous advertising campaigns in the 1960s.

In later life, having had a cancerous tumour removed, he became an anti-smoking campaigner.

McLean died of lung cancer. A year later his family brought a lawsuit against Marlboro manufacturers Phillip Morris. The case is still pending.

WESTMINSTER DAVIDS

The son of English philosopher **David Hartley** (1705-1757), **David Hartley, the younger** (1732-1813) was MP for Kingston-upon-Hull. In 1783 he and Benjamin Franklin drew up and signed the Treaty of Paris, which formally ended the American Revolutionary War between Great Britain and the USA. He was also the first MP to put the case for abolition of the slave trade before the House of Commons.

"...the slave trade is contrary to the laws of God and the rights of men"
David Hartley

David Mellor (b. 1949) was never far from controversy during a Westminster career that began when he entered Parliament as Conservative MP for Putney in 1979. He was probably best known – politically at least – for his time as head of the Department of National Heritage, which became jokingly known as 'The Ministry of Fun'.

However, it was around this time that he was involved in a kiss-and-tell scandal. To add spice to the lurid tabloid revelations, publicist Max Clifford allegedly concocted the story that Mellor had asked the actress involved, Antonia de Sancha, to make love to him whilst he was wearing his Chelsea FC football kit. To put what seemed the final nail in his political coffin, it also emerged that he had enjoyed a free holiday as the guest of a daughter of a Palestine Liberation Organisation official, and yet another holiday paid for by the ruler of Abu Dhabi. Mellor duly resigned. However, he did return to Westminster as chairman of the incoming Labour government's Football Task Force in 1997.

"Since the great days of Jimmy Greaves, it's the only time anyone's managed to score five times in a Chelsea shirt"
Tony Banks MP, fellow Chelsea fan, after the revelations about his affair with actress Antonia de Sancha

David Blunkett (b. 1947) was leader of Sheffield Council between 1980 and 1987, and during his tenure the city administration was regularly denounced for its so-called 'Loony Left' policies, whilst becoming known as 'The People's Republic of South Yorkshire'.

A decade after becoming an MP, Blunkett was appointed Education Secretary in Tony Blair's first Cabinet of 1997, and thus becoming the first blind Cabinet minister in UK history. He became Home Secretary in 2001 and resigned three years later following a paternity scandal involving an American-born publisher.

However, having returned in 2005 and taken up the role of Secretary of State for Work and Pensions, he was again forced to resign after reports about his external business interests. He has, to date, had five guide dogs by his side in the House of Commons. One of them, a black Labrador named Lucy, once vomited during a speech by Conservative opposition member **David Willetts** (b. 1956).

SOME MIDDLE NAME DAVIDS

Rod Stewart
– born Roderick David Stewart in 1945

Sculptor Antony Gormley
– born Antony Mark David Gormley in 1950

HRH Prince Harry
– born Henry Charles Albert David Mountbatten Windsor in 1984

Edward VIII
– born Edward Albert Christian George Andrew Patrick David Windsor in 1894

Singer/songwriter John Martyn
– born as Iain David McGeachy in 1948

Catcher in the Rye novelist J. D. Salinger
– born Jerome David Salinger in 1919

Murderer of John Lennon, Mark David Chapman
– born in 1955. He was carrying a copy of *Catcher in the Rye* at the time...

HOLLYWOOD DAVIDS

The son of the Confederate Army Civil War hero 'Roaring Jake' Griffith, **David Wark (DW) Griffith** (1875-1948) would become arguably the first true craftsman of the cinema. In 1910 whist working with the Biograph Company, Griffith began filming in a 'little village' where the weather was good, the people were friendly and there was room for growth. That 'village' was Hollywood. His major works included the controversial 1915 film *The Birth of a Nation*, and *Intolerance*, which was released the following year. Griffith co-founded United Artists in 1919 along with Charlie Chaplin, Mary Pickford, and Douglas Fairbanks, but he would never again match the box office of his previous films.

"The teacher of us all"
Charlie Chaplin on DW Griffith

David O. Selznick (1902-1965) not only introduced American filmgoers to Fred Astaire, Katharine Hepburn, Ingrid Bergman, Vivien Leigh and Alfred Hitchcock, but also produced back-to-back Oscar winning movies, *Gone with the Wind* (1939), and *Rebecca* (1940). His 1946 epic, *Duel in the Sun*, was one of the first films that influenced Martin Scorsese to become a director. Selznick was an obsessive memo-sender, and it is alleged that he recorded his every thought from 1916 to his death in memos that filled 2,000 file boxes.

"The way I see it, my function is to be responsible for everything"
David O. Selznick

CLASSIC BRITISH FILM DAVIDS

David Lean (1908-1991) was responsible for some of the greatest British movies ever made including;

In Which We Serve (1942)
This Happy Breed (1944)
Blithe Spirit (1945)
Brief Encounter (1945)
Great Expectations (1946)
Oliver Twist (1948)
The Sound Barrier (1952)
Hobson's Choice (1954)
The Bridge on the River Kwai (1957) – Oscar winner
Lawrence of Arabia (1962) – Oscar winner
Doctor Zhivago (1965)
Ryan's Daughter (1970)
A Passage to India (1984)

"If you have no hope of getting one, they're despised. But if you have, they're very important"
David Lean on the Oscars

———◆———

MURDERED DAVIDS

A privileged background could not bolster the career of American actor **David Bacon** (1914-1943). The legendary Howard Hughes, a rumoured lover of Bacon's, cast him as *The Masked Marvel* in a low-budget film serial of the same name. But shortly after Bacon had completed filming, he was found in his crashed car wearing only a pair of swimming trunks.

He had a knife embedded in his back. A camera found in the car revealed only one image – that of the naked and smiling Bacon on a beach. Police suspected that the photograph had been taken by the killer shortly before, but the crime was never solved. His Austrian wife, Greta Keller, a would-be film actress, would later reveal that both she and her husband were gay, and that the marriage merely served to give them a respectable Hollywood appearance. Keller would later become a popular cabaret singer and, in 1972, her voice appeared in the Oscar-winning film *Cabaret*, in which she sang Married.

<hr />

FINAL RESTING PLACE DAVY

To be sent to **'Davy Jones's Locker'** is a euphemism for death at sea and the 'locker' is the resting place of drowned sailors. Though who Davy Jones actually was is open to debate, an early reference appeared in Tobias Smollett's 1751 novel, *The Adventures of Peregrine Pickle*. Davy Jones is also referenced in classic novels such as Washington Irving's *Adventures of the Black Fisherman*, Herman Melville's *Moby Dick*, Robert Louis Stevenson's *Treasure Island* and J. M. Barrie's *Peter and Wendy*. He is also regularly referenced in Nickelodeon's popular animated series *SpongeBob SquarePants*

PIRATICAL DAVIDS

Jean-David Nau (1635-1668), better known as François l'Olonnais, was a French pirate. Most legends attest to his cruelty, including the tale of the time he pillaged a city where the inhabitants had fled after hiding their treasures. They were eventually tracked town and tortured one-by-one until they gave up the location of their possessions. L'Olonnais' death was equally barbaric – he was eaten alive by a tribe of Native Americans.

"He drew his cutlass, and with it cut open the breast of one of those poor Spaniards, and pulling out his heart with his sacrilegious hands, began to bite and gnaw it with his teeth, like a ravenous wolf, saying to the rest: 'I will serve you all alike, if you show me not another way'."
Descriptive example of **Jean-David Nau**'s ruthlessness

Loosely based on the old sailors' legend, **Davy Jones** is a fictional character that appears in the *Pirates of the Caribbean* film series. In the movies, the notorious Jones (Bill Nighy) captains the ghost ship *Flying Dutchman*, which sails the seas in search of lost souls to serve on-board. Before Nighy was cast, the producers also saw Jim Broadbent, Iain Glenn and Richard E. Grant.

"Life is cruel. Why should the afterlife be any different?"
Davy Jones: Pirates of the Caribbean: Dead Man's Chest

The Times Rich List Davids 2008

10th **David and Simon Reuben** (Property etc.) £4,300m

21st **David Khalili** (Art and property) £2,500m

40th **Sir David and Sir Frederick Barclay** (Property and media) £1,700m

47th **Alki David** and the Leventis family (Industry) £1,500m

60th Lady Grantchester and **David Moores** and family (Retail and football pools) £1,200m

87th **David Ross** (Property and mobile phones) £873m

100th **David Bromilow** (Sports goods and media) £755m

112th **David Wilson** and family (Construction) £729m

113th **Sir David Murray** (Property and football) £720m

117th **Jonathan and David Rowland** (Finance) £700m

Stadium Filler Davids

Born in east London, guitarist **David Evans**'s (b. 1961) family moved to Ireland when he was aged just one. At secondary school he became part of a band called Feedback alongside **Paul David Hewson** (b. 1960) and Larry Mullen Jr.

This band became The Hype and, in 1978 metamorphosised into U2. Hewson became 'Bono' and Evans became known as 'The Edge'. Considerable speculation has surrounded how he got the name. Bono stated that he loves to walk close to the edges of buildings and very high walls. The other reason offered is that the name originated because of his angular facial features. Apart from his unique guitar style, his other signature feature is his headgear. Evans's hair began thinning in his early twenties and he is rarely seen without some kind of head covering.

<hr/>

SOME NAME CHANGE DAVIDS

Ricky 'Tell Laura I Love Her' Valance was born **David Spencer** in 1939

John le Carré was born **David John Moore Cornwell** in 1931

Danny Kaye was born **David Daniel Kaminsky** in 1913

American rapper **David Banner** was born Levell Crump in 1973

Jude Law was born **David Jude Heyworth Law** in 1972

Lou 'Mambo No. 5' Bega was born **David Lubega** in 1975

Ziggy Marley was born **David Nesta Marley** in 1968

Classical actor Paul Scofield was born **David Paul Scofield** in 1922

David *'Kung Fu'* **Carradine** was born John Arthur Carradine in 1936

Harold Pinter used the stage name **David Baron** in the mid-1950s.

TREKKIE DAVIDS

In 1966, whilst still a student, Chicago-born **David Gerrold** (b. 1944) submitted a number of storylines to the brand new sci-fi series *Star Trek*. The story the producers chose was *The Trouble with Tribbles* which became one of the most popular episodes from the original series.

The 3ft 11ins. tall **David Rappaport** (1951-1990) was one of the most recognisable dwarf actors in British TV and film. In the 1980s he made frequent appearances as 'Shades' in the cult Saturday morning TV show *Tiswas*. This was followed by his best-known film role as Randall in Terry Gilliam's *Time Bandits*. Struggling with depression, he committed suicide at the age of just 39. Rappaport's death was one of the primary reasons Terry Gilliam shelved the sequel to *Time Bandits*, as his character was central to the story. At the time of his death Rappaport was filming a guest spot on *Star Trek: The Next Generation*.

British TV director **David Carson** cut his teeth on such popular series as *Crown Court, Coronation Street, Sherlock Holmes* and *Bergerac* before taking his talent to the USA where he went on to direct shows such as *Smallville, Doogie Howser, M.D., LA Law* and episodes of *Star Trek: The Next Generation* and *Star Trek: Deep Space Nine*. He also directed the feature film *Star Trek Generations* in 1994.

David Farragut (1801-1870) became the first full admiral
of the U.S. Navy, and contributed greatly to the Union
victory in the American Civil War. His greatest triumph was
in the Battle of Mobile Bay in 1864. Heavily protected by
mines (or 'torpedoes', as they were then known) the bay was
the last Confederacy port still in operation on the Gulf of
Mexico. But the aggressive Farragut forced his way through.
A year later he was a pallbearer at the funeral of President
Abraham Lincoln. Five U.S. Navy destroyers have been
named in his honour, and there have also been three USS
Farragut's in *Star Trek*. On top of this, a character called
Commodore Farragut appeared in Jules Verne's 1870 novel
Twenty Thousand Leagues Under the Sea.

"Damn the torpedoes, full speed ahead!"
David Farragut's alleged battle cry at the Battle of
Mobile Bay

British stage actor **David Warner** (b. 1941) has had a
career dotted with coincidences, usually pertaining to the
number three. He has appeared in three movies about the
Titanic: *S.O.S. Titanic* (1979), *Time Bandits* (1981) and *Titanic*
(1997). He played an ape in *Planet of the Apes* (2001), was
obsessed with gorillas in his 'breakthrough' film *Morgan: A
Suitable Case for Treatment* (1966) and he did an impression of
a gorilla in *The Man with Two Brains* (1983).

As well as this, he has appeared in three films that involve
time travel: *Time After Time* (1979), *Time Bandits* (1981) and
Planet of the Apes (2001). And if that was not enough, he has
also played three different species in *Star Trek*: a human in

Star Trek V: The Final Frontier (1989), a Klingon in *Star Trek VI: The Undiscovered Country* (1991) and a Cardassian in *Star Trek: The Next Generation* (1987). Warner has also played The Doctor in audio versions of *Dr. Who*.

In 1967 Leonard Nimoy (Mr. Spock) was in a contract dispute with the producers of *Star Trek*. One of the actors considered to replace him was **David Canary** (b. 1938). However, the dispute was resolved. Canary went on to star as ranch foreman Candy Canaday in the western series *Bonanza*, and as both Adam Chandler and his twin brother Stuart in over four hundred episodes of *All My Children*. He is the great great nephew of Martha Jane Canary – better known as 19th century frontierswoman Calamity Jane.

<hr>

1950s HEARTTHROB DAVIDS

Born in Hull, and a veteran of the 1944 D-Day landings in France, **David Whitfield** (1925-1980) became a pre-rock 'n' roll pin-up with his swoon-inducing operatic style. His popularity on both sides of the Atlantic was confirmed by a string of hits, an appearance on the *Ed Sullivan Show*, and a summons to be one of the stars in the 1954 Royal Command Performance.

Also in that year, he became one of only six artists to have spent ten or more consecutive weeks at number one in the UK with Cara Mia. Inevitably his appeal diminished with the advent of rock 'n' roll.

INTERNATIONAL RUGBY DAVIDS WITH MORE THAN 50 CAPS

David Campese (Australia) - 101 caps between 1982 and 1996

David Humphreys (Ireland) - 70 caps between 1996 and 2006

David Wallace (Ireland) - 52 caps between 2000 and 2009*

David Giffin (Australia) - 50 caps between 1996 and 2003

David Young (Wales) - 51 caps between 1987 and 2001

(still playing)*

FRONTIER DAVY

On his tombstone it states that **Davy Crockett** (1786-1836) was a pioneer, patriot, soldier, trapper, explorer, state legislator, Congressman – and that he was martyred at The Alamo.

Colonel David Crockett was also one of America's greatest folk heroes. Having served in the military, he was elected to represent Tennessee in the US House of Representatives and, as a Congressman, he ultimately failed in his opposition of President Jackson's policy of removing Native Americans from their land, in what became the Indian Removal Act of 1830.

Crockett was killed at the Battle of the Alamo when 6,000 Mexicans attacked Texan forces numbering no more than 250. Both John Wayne and Billy Bob Thornton have portrayed Crockett in movies, and three different versions of the song, **The Ballad of Davy Crockett**, were released in 1955.

"Be always sure you are right, then go ahead"
Davy Crockett

———◆———

FOULMOUTHED FOOTBALLING DAVE

Whilst playing for Forfar Athletic in 2000, tough-tackling former Scottish international **David 'Psycho' Bowman** (b. 1964) was banned for seven games after effectively being given a total of four red cards in a game against Berwick Rangers.

"The player has been reported for being sent off, originally for two cautions. But he has also been reported for using foul and abusive language on three separate occasions and this amounts to another three orderings off, giving a total of four"
A Scottish Football Association official

The Simpsons Special Guest Davids

Michael McKean as **David St. Hubbins** (*Spinal Tap*)
David Crosby (Crosby, Stills, Nash & Young) as himself
David Duchovny as Fox Mulder (*X-Files*)
David Hyde Pierce (*Frasier*) as Cecil Terwilliger
Dave Thomas (*Grace Under Fire*) as Rex Banner
David Lander (*Laverne & Shirley*) as Squiggy
David Byrne (*Talking Heads*) as himself

Piano Playing David

A child prodigy at the piano, at 19 years of age **David Helfgott** (b. 1947) won a scholarship to study at the Royal College of Music in London. It was during this time that he began to exhibit manifestations of a mental illness, which would later be diagnosed as schizoaffective disorder.

Much of the 1970s was spent in virtual obscurity in his home country of Australia. However, having met his future wife Gillian, he made a triumphant return to the concert circuit in the 1980s. Helfgott's life story became the film *Shine* (1996), starring Geoffrey Rush in an Oscar-winning performance.

INDUSTRIAL NEW WAVE DAVE

In 1980 **Dave Gahan** (b. 1962) became lead singer with influential electronic band Depeche Mode. On the back of such hits as Just Can't Get Enough, See You, and Everything Counts, Gahan stumbled from excess to excess and by the 1990s appeared to be in a losing battle with his heroin addiction.

By 1995 there were rumours that he was spending twelve hours a day inside a wardrobe whilst watching the Weather Channel and talking to a Tin Man doll. A suicide attempt followed that he later stated was more of a cry for help. A year later, having overdosed on a lethal speedball cocktail of heroin and cocaine, he was clinically dead for two minutes, but then revived by paramedics.

SOME FOOTBALL MANAGER DAVIDS

Dave Sexton (b. 1930): Leyton Orient, Chelsea, QPR, Manchester United, England U-21s and Coventry City
Dave Mackay (b. 1934): Swindon, Nottingham Forest, Derby County, Walsall, Kuwait, Doncaster Rovers, Birmingham City and Zamalek
Dave Bassett (b. 1944): Wimbledon, Watford, Sheffield United, Crystal Palace, Nottingham Forest, Barnsley and Leicester City
David Pleat (b. 1945): Luton Town, Spurs, Leicester City and Sheffield Wednesday
David Webb (b. 1946): AFC Bournemouth, Torquay United, Southend United, Chelsea, Brentford and Yeovil

Dave Jones (b. 1956): Stockport County, Southampton, Wolves and Cardiff City
David O'Leary (b. 1958): Leeds United and Aston Villa
David Moyes (b. 1963): Preston North End and Everton

⫘⬦⬦⫘

A COUPLE OF UK FILM DAVIDS

In 1982 screenwriter **David Leland** (b. 1947) teamed up with director Alan Clarke to create *Made In England* – the TV film that first brought actor Tim Roth to public attention. At the forefront of a resurgent British film industry he went on to write the 1986 thriller *Mona Lisa*. He followed this a year later with *Personal Services*, along with his directorial debut *Wish You Were Here* for which he won a Best Screenplay BAFTA.

Other work has included *The Land Girls* which he co-wrote and directed, and directing an episode of the multi award winning World War II epic *Band of Brothers*.

David Yates (b. 1963) was first inspired to be a director when he saw Steven Spielberg's *Jaws*, and he was given his first camera at the age of 14. Having worked extensively in British TV, he has since become deeply involved in the Harry Potter canon – directing *The Order of the Phoenix* and *The Half-Blood Prince*. Yates is also due to direct the final two-part instalment, *Harry Potter and the Deathly Hallows*.

Religious Davids

The **Star of David** is the symbol most commonly associated with Judaism. It first gained popularity when it was adopted as the emblem of the Zionist movement in 1897. When the modern state of Israel was born in 1948, it was incorporated into the national flag. One theory to the exact origins of the symbol is that it represents King David's shield and, to save metal, leather was stretched over a simple hexagonal frame. In the 17th century, the Star of David was often seen on the outside of synagogues, to identify them as Jewish houses of worship. In Nazi Germany all Jews wore the 'yellow star'.

The late 17th century was a bad time to be a Catholic in England and Wales. There was fear and hysteria concerning an alleged conspiracy to assassinate Charles II, and a growing belief amongst Protestants that Catholics were gaining extensive influence. This became known as the Popish Plot and amongst its many victims was **David Lewis** (1616-1679).

Born a Protestant in Wales but converting to Catholicism in his teens, he worked in his homeland for thirty years before being arrested in 1678, and brought to trial on charges of being a Catholic priest, high treason, and an accessory to the Popish Plot. He was hanged, drawn, and quartered a year later. Lewis was canonised as a saint by Pope Paul VI in 1970.

Allegedly born on a cliff top during a violent storm, **Saint David** (c. 500–589) became the patron saint of Wales. He died on March 1st, which is now celebrated as **St David's Day**. In his lifetime he was renowned as both teacher and preacher, and founded monastic settlements and churches in Wales, Cornwall and Brittany. A legend exists that once, whilst he was delivering a sermon, the crowd at the back could not see him.

It was then that the ground on which he was standing rose up to form a hill so that everyone had a good view. The village of Llanddewi Brefi is said to stand on the spot where this miracle occurred.

Llanddewi Brefi is also home to *Little Britain* character, **Daffyd 'I'm the only gay in the village' Thomas.**

FORMULA ONE DRIVING DAVIDS

David Hampshire (GB) 2 starts in 1950
David Murray (GB) 4 starts between 1950 and 1952
David Piper (GB) 2 starts between 1959 and 1960
David Prophet (GB) 2 starts between 1963 and 1965
David Hobbs (GB) 7 starts between 1967 and 1974
Dave Charlton (South Africa) 11 starts between 1967 and 1975
Dave Walker (Australia) 11 starts between 1971 and 1972
David Purley (GB) 7 starts between 1973 and 1977
Dave Morgan (GB) 1 start in 1975
David Brabham (Australia) 24 starts between 1990 and 1994
David Coulthard (GB) 246 starts and 13 wins between 1994 and 2008

GREEN CROSS CODE DAVID

Bristol-born bodybuilder and actor **David Prowse** (b. 1935) is probably best known for two roles; firstly as the 1970s superhero and children's road safety supremo The Green Cross Code Man, and secondly as the physical form of Darth Vader (voiced by James Earl Jones) in the original *Star Wars* trilogy. Carrie Fisher, who played Princess Leia, is said to have nicknamed him 'Darth Farmer' because of his broad West Country accent.

An ex-Commonwealth Games weightlifter, Prowse has spent his acting career playing mostly 'strong-arm' or monster roles in films such as *A Clockwork Orange*, *The People That Time Forgot*, *The Horror of Frankenstein* and *Vampire Circus*.

He also helped train Christopher Reeve for the role of *Superman*.

◆

PSYCHEDELIC DAVID

American pharmacologist **David E. Nichols** (b. 1944) has been legitimately researching the chemistry of psychedelic drugs since the late 1960s, and, amongst his peers, is considered to be one of the foremost experts on the subject. In 2004 Nichols delivered a lecture for the International Serotonin Club entitled *35 years studying psychedelics: what a long strange trip it's been*.

◆

SOME LAURENCE OLIVIER AWARD-WINNING DAVIDS

David Edgar (Best New Play): *The Life and Adventures of Nicholas Nickleby* 1980 (Adaptation from Charles Dickens' novel)
David Mamet (Best New Play): *Glengarry Glen Ross* 1983
David Hare (Best New Play): *Racing Demon* 1990
David Hirson (Best New Comedy): *La Bete* 1992
David Bamber (Best Actor): *My Night with Reg* 1995
David Atkins (Best Theatre Choreographer): *Hot Shoe Shuffle* 1995 (shared with Dein Perry)
David Hare (Best New Play): *Skylight* 1996
David Bedella (Best Actor in a Musical): *Jerry Springer – The Opera* 2004
David Harrower (Best New Play): *Blackbird* 2007

Dr. Who Davids

David Morrissey (b. 1964) played the 'pretend' Doctor, Jackson Lake, in the 2008 Christmas special.

David Gooderson (b. 1941) played Dr. Who's greatest advisory, Davros, in the 1979 adventure *Destiny of the Daleks*. He had, however, begun his career in slightly more refined circles, as Vice-President of Cambridge Footlights in 1963. Other Footlight members that year included Graeme Garden, Eric Idle, Jonathan Lynn, Richard Eyre and Bill Oddie.

Davros – a possible derivation of 'David' – is the crippled megalomaniac creator of the Daleks.

His modest ambition is to be the supreme being and ruler of the universe.

This son of a Presbyterian minister started life as **David McDonald** (b. 1971) but because there was already an actor with that name – and inspired by an article he was reading about Neil Tennant from the Pet Shop Boys – he changed his name to **David Tennant.** He was already an established theatre actor when cast as the young *Casanova* (to Peter O'Toole's older version) in the TV series of the same name. In fact the writer of that series, Russell T. Davies, was so impressed with his performance that he then cast him in the role of The Doctor. He is only the second Scotsman to play the role, the first being Sylvester McCoy.

David Whitaker (1928-1980) not only wrote for the series in the early days, he also acted as story or script editor for over fifty episodes including the very first entitled: *An Unearthly Child*.

When in 1989, *Doctor Who – The Ultimate Adventure* toured Britain as a stage show, the cast was led by the third incarnation of the Doctor, John Pertwee. **David Banks** (b. 1951), having already appeared as a Cyberleader in several episodes of the TV series, played Karl, a mercenary who is in league with both the Daleks and the Cybermen. However, for two performances in Birmingham he took over the role of The Doctor when Pertwee fell ill.

In the 1966 film *Daleks' Invasion Earth: 2150 AD*, one of the main resistance fighters was named **David**, and played by Ray *Mr Benn* Brooks.

David Collings (b. 1940) has appeared as Vorus in *Revenge of the Cybermen*, Mawdryn in *Mawdryn Undead* and Poul in *The Robots of Death*.

David Ellis (d. 1978) co-wrote – with Malcolm Hulke – *The Faceless Ones* for the 1967 serial starring The Doctor's second incarnation, Patrick Troughton. Ellis also wrote episodes of *Dixon of Dock Green* and *Z Cars*.

In 1965 **David Maloney** (1933-2006) became a
production assistant on *Dr. Who*, but would eventually go
on to direct over forty episodes between 1968 and 1977.
Although he did other notable work for the BBC including
When the Boat Comes In and *Last of the Mohicans*, he often
gravitated to sci-fi.

As a producer he oversaw the first three series of *Blake's 7* in
the late 1970s and early 1980s, and was responsible for the
1981 BBC adaptation of John Wyndham's novel *The Day of
the Triffids*.

⊰━◆━⊱

A Couple of Ruling Davids

David I (1085-1153) King of Scotland from 1124 to his
death
David II (1324-1371) King of Scotland from 1329 to his
death

HARD ROCKING DAVID

In the 1960s Manny Roth ran a New York club called Café
Wha?, where up-and-coming acts such as Bob Dylan and
Jimi Hendrix played early gigs. Often amongst the hip
Greenwich Village audience was Manny's pre-teen nephew
David Lee Roth (b. 1955), who would go on to become
lead singer with Van Halen.

*"Money can't buy you happiness, but it can buy you a yacht big enough
to pull up right alongside it."*
David Lee Roth

SNAPPY DAVIDS

'Chim' – a mispronunciation of his Polish birth name,
Szymin – was the pseudonym of photojournalist **David
Seymour** (1911-1956). Having covered the Spanish Civil
War, Seymour enlisted in the U.S. Army, going on to serve in
Europe as a photo interpreter during World War II. It was in
1942, the same year that his parents were killed by the Nazis,
that he became a naturalised American citizen, and in 1947
he, Robert Capa and Henri Cartier-Bresson co-founded
Magnum, the world famous photographers' cooperative.

Also noted for his later work in photographing Hollywood
stars such as Sophia Loren and Kirk Douglas, Chim's life
was ended by Egyptian machine-gun fire whilst covering the
Suez War.

While at university in Arizona, future photojournalist **David Duncan** (b. 1916) took pictures of a burning hotel, and in particular one man who went back into the building to retrieve his suitcase. The man turned out to be notorious bank robber John Dillinger and the suitcase contained the proceeds from a bank robbery. Duncan's pictures became newsworthy. He went on to become a combat photographer covering World War II in the South Pacific as well as conflicts in Turkey, Eastern Europe, Africa and the Middle East, but is perhaps best known for his work during the Korean and Vietnam Wars.

<hr />

SOME INTERNATIONAL FOOTBALLING DAVIDS

David Beckham (England): 108 caps & 17 goals – 1996 to 2009*
David Seaman (England): 75 caps & 0 goals – 1988 to 2002
David O'Leary (Republic of Ireland): 68 caps & 1 goal – 1976 to 1993
David McCreery (Northern Ireland): 67 caps & no goals – 1976 to 1990
David Healy (Northern Ireland): 66 caps & 35 goals – 2000 to 2009*
Dave Watson (England): 65 caps & 4 goals – 1974 to 1982
David Weir (Scotland): 63 caps & 1 goal – 1998 to 2008
David Platt (England): 62 caps & 27 goals – 1989 to 1996
David Phillips (Wales): 62 caps & 0 goals – 1982 to 1996
Dai Davies (Wales): 52 caps & 0 goals – 1975 to 1983

CHAT SHOW DAVID

Comedy/chat show host **David Letterman** (b. 1947)
began his career on local radio in Indianapolis before
becoming 'anchor' and weatherman on a local TV station.
During this time he upped his profile with offbeat, on-air
behaviour – on one occasion congratulating a tropical storm
on being upgraded to a hurricane. Letterman has been a
staple of late-night viewing in the US since 1982, and is
second only to his great influence Johnny Carson in TV
chat-longevity. When Carson retired after 30 years' service
on *The Tonight Show*, both Letterman and his great rival Jay
Leno vied for the slot, with Leno winning. *The Late Shift* was
a 1996 film based on the battle for the coveted spot, with
Letterman being played by John Michael Higgins.

*"Nothing, believe me, nothing is more satisfying to me personally than
getting a great idea and then beating it to death"*
David Letterman

METEOROLOGICAL DAVID

In 1979, **Hurricane David**, with winds of up to 175 mph, became one of the deadliest hurricanes of the late 20th century killing over 2,000 people, primarily in the Dominican Republic. David was only the second male name used for a tropical storm.

⚍⬥⚌

BIBLICAL MOVIE DAVID

According to the Old Testament **King David** (c. 1037-967 BC) was the second king of Israel, reigning over Judah for seven years and over Judah and Israel for a further thirty-three years. Although there is little archaeological evidence to support the Bible depiction, his story is profoundly important to both Jewish and Christian culture. It was the young Israelite David who slayed the Philistine giant Goliath with a stone from his slingshot. David has been portrayed on film by the likes of Gregory Peck, Finlay Currie, Keith Michell and Richard Gere.

⚍⬥⚌

ARTISTIC DAVIDS

The Whitechapel Boys were a group of Anglo-Jewish writers and artists who came from, or lived around, this area of east London. Amongst their number was **David Bomberg** (1890-1957). He was expelled from the Slade School of Art in 1913 for what was seen as a breach of convention – his work often involving complex geometric construction, heavily influenced by the cubist and futurist movements.

His style has, in fact, been likened to the New York Graffiti movement of the 1970s, his figures often being created out of hard-edged 3D shapes. Although he died in 1957, it was over thirty years before his work was given a major retrospective at the Tate Gallery.

Bradford-born **David Hockney** (b. 1937) is revered as one of the most influential British artists of the 20th century. It was whilst still a student at the Royal College of Art that Hockney's work appeared in the 1961 ICA Young Contemporaries exhibition which effectively announced the arrival of British 'Pop Art'. He went on to make a name for himself in the USA where his acrylic paintings of Californian swimming pools became immensely popular.

Hockney would go on to diversify into photomontage and portraiture as well as designing for the stage. Much of his work has had more than a hint of homo-eroticism and early in his career he illustrated this with a work entitled *Doll Boy* which was based on a crush he had on pop singer Cliff Richard.

"All art is contemporary, if it's alive. And if it's not alive, what's the point of it?"
David Hockney

Leading Scottish contemporary sculptor and installation artist **David Mach** (b. 1956) has frequently used mass-produced objects to create his work. These include anything from newspapers and magazines to house bricks. Many of his pieces are constructed in public spaces. His *'Brick Train'* – a depiction of a steam engine made from 185,000 bricks – was constructed near a supermarket outside Darlington.

At the other end of the scale, Mach has built human or animal heads from unstruck matchsticks. However, having once accidentally set fire to one of these heads, he now ignites his matches before construction as a form of performance art. Having been nominated for the Turner Prize in 1988, he became Professor of Sculpture at the Royal Academy of Arts in 2000.

'PIPE SMOKER OF THE YEAR' DAVIDS

Dave Lee Travis 1982
David Bryant 1986

REVISIONIST DAVIDS

Having been a lecturer at the University of Munich, American historian **David Hoggan** (1923-1988) went on to become a trailblazer for the Holocaust denial industry in the 1960s. Amongst his published theories were that the Polish government had engaged in the persecution of its German minority and that the outbreak of World War II was due to an alleged Anglo-Polish conspiracy to wage aggression against Germany. He also claimed that Hitler's foreign policy was entirely peaceful and moderate, and Germany was the innocent victim of Allied aggression.

David Irving (b. 1938) is a controversial British historian. Although already established as a Third Reich and Holocaust revisionist, he first came to wider public attention in 1983 when it was claimed by leading war historian Hugh Trevor-Roper that the recently discovered *Hitler Diaries* were the genuine article. Irving, correctly as it turned out, initially denounced them as forgeries. However, his known right-wing extremism has always clouded his reputation as an historian.

An example of this was when, in 1996, he brought an unsuccessful libel case against American historian Deborah Lipstadt and Penguin Books. During the trial the court found that Irving was an active Holocaust denier, as well as an anti-Semite and racist.

"…Irving was motivated by a desire to present events in a manner consistent with his own ideological beliefs even if that involved distortion and manipulation of historical evidence"
Justice Gray – part of his judgement at the 'Irving v Lipstadt' libel trial in 1996

DUPLICATING DAVID

Towards the end of the 19th century, the young Hungarian-born **David Gestetner** (1854-1939) moved to Vienna to work in the stock market. One of his duties at the end of trading was the tedious task of making copies of the day's activities – by hand.

So Gestetner invented the very first method of reproducing documents quickly and inexpensively, and thus became the pioneer of office automation. The Gestetner stencil duplicator became an overnight sensation, with a system that involved waxed paper, his patented 'Cyclostyle' writing stylus, and ink rollers. Gestetner moved to London and opened a factory in 1906, which, until the 1970s, employed up to 6,000 people.

DUAL CODE RUGBY INTERNATIONAL DAVIDS

David Jones (Wales): Union debut versus England 1902; League debut versus New Zealand All Golds 1908
Dave Valentine (Scotland): Union debut versus Ireland 1947; League debut Great Britain versus Australia 1948
David Watkins (Wales): Union debut versus England 1963; League debut Great Britain versus Australia 1973

A Couple of Top Shelf Davids

English businessman **David Gold**'s (b. 1937) first contact with publishing came when he was running a small pulp-novel kiosk just off London's Charing Cross Road, where he soon discovered that the big money was in the more salacious and erotic end of the market.

Thus, an empire was born. Gold went on to own a chain of 'top-shelf' magazines, as well as tabloid newspapers. Gold Group International, formed with his brother Ralph, has since diversified into such well-known high street retailers as Ann Summers and Knickerbox. Gold's other passions are aviation and football. A useful player as a youngster – he netted the winning goal for London Youth against their Glasgow counterparts in front of 12,000 people at Selhurst Park – Gold became co-owner and chairman of Birmingham City.

The chairman of Birmingham City's parent company, Birmingham City plc, is another man who made his fortune in the print and pornography industry. At the age of 21 **David Sullivan** (b. 1949) was making up to £800 a week by selling sheets of pornographic photographs by mail order. By the mid-seventies, he controlled half the adult magazine market in Britain, and towards the end of that decade he was producing low-budget sex movies, which starred his then-girlfriend Mary Millington. His greatest publishing rivals were, ironically, the Gold brothers. Sullivan suggested they join forces and in 1986 they launched the innovative *Daily Sport* and *Sunday Sport* tabloid newspaper.

"I've only got one car – a Bentley – because I don't want that problem of 'what car shall I drive today?'"
David Sullivan

LYRICAL BROTHER DAVIDS

The **Mack David** (1912-1993) lyric for La Vie en Rose – performed by Louis Armstrong – was heard fifteen years after his death in the Pixar animation blockbuster *Wall-E*. Mack, unlike his younger brother Hal, was best known for his work in film, where he was nominated eight times for an Oscar.

Amongst his musical collaborators were Henry Mancini on the 1961 movie *Bachelor in Paradise*, and Elmer Bernstein on firstly the 1962 release *Walk on the Wild Side* – the first Hollywood film to openly feature lesbianism – and then the 1966 film *Hawaii*, one of the earliest movies to feature a Moog synthesizer in its score.

Influential song-writing team, composer Burt Bacharach and lyricist **Hal David** (b. 1921), came up with some of the most enduring songs in American popular music.

"When I hear music, very often I hear a story. The fact that it was Tulsa, as opposed to Dallas, is not terribly meaningful, but the sound of 'Tulsa' rang in my ear."
Hal David on writing the lyrics for 24 Hours From Tulsa

Ten Songs Co-witten by Hal David

24 Hours From Tulsa
Trains and Boat and Planes
Do You Know The Way To San Jose?
Walk On By
Always Something There To Remind Me
Close To You
What's New Pussycat?
Alfie
The Look Of Love
Raindrops Keep Fallin' On My Head

———⋙◆⋘———

Party Leader Davids

Although born in Manchester, **David Lloyd George** (1863-1945) moved to Wales with his mother when his father died. Deeply proud of his Welsh heritage, he became a Liberal MP in 1890 and would go on to be at the forefront of the Liberal Reforms, which included the introduction of old age pensions, unemployment benefit and state support for the sick.

Lloyd George was vehemently opposed to the Boer War, but changed his stance on the outbreak of World War I, and in 1916 he became Prime Minister of a coalition government becoming the last Liberal to hold the office. In 1921 he presided over the establishment of the Irish Free State and a year later was involved in a scandal that had involved the sale of knighthoods and peerages.

However, rather than pure profiteering, his motives were to use the money to create a party comprising moderate Liberals and Conservatives. This indiscretion effectively ended his tenure as Prime Minister.

"Don't be afraid to take a big step if one is indicated. You can't cross a chasm in two small jumps."
David Lloyd George

David Ben-Gurion (1886-1973) was the first Prime Minister of Israel and, except for a two-year period in the 1950s, led the country from 1948 to 1963. Born David Grün in Poland, which was then part of the Russian Empire, he was a passionate Zionist and went to Palestine in 1906 where he became involved in the establishment of the first agricultural workers commune, which would later evolve into the kibbutz.

It was while studying law at Istanbul University that he adopted the Hebrew name of Ben-Gurion – named after a medieval Jewish historian called Yosef ben Gurion. As Prime Minister he was the driving force behind many state institutions, and also oversaw 'Operation Magic Carpet', which involved the 1949 airlift of some 50,000 Jews from Arab countries.

"In Israel, in order to be a realist you must believe in miracles"
David Ben-Gurion

In 1998 Ulster Unionist Party leader **David Trimble**
(b. 1944), along with Social Democratic and Labour
Party leader John Hume, were awarded the Nobel Peace
Prize following the Belfast 'Good Friday' Agreement –
an attempt to find a peaceful solution to the ongoing
troubles in Northern Ireland. As a consequence Trimble
became First Minister in the newly formed devolved
government.

*"There are two traditions in Northern Ireland. There are two main
religious denominations. But there is only one true moral denomination.
And it wants peace"*
David Trimble

David Cameron (b. 1966) is a direct descendant of
King William IV and his mistress, Dorothy Jordan, who
together had in the region of ten illegitimate children. As a
consequence, this makes him the fifth cousin, twice removed
of Queen Elizabeth II. First elected to Parliament in 2001,
his rise to the leadership of the Conservative party was
swift and by 2005 he was slugging it out for the top job with
David Davis (b. 1948), winning the contest on the second
ballot. It is alleged that he is called 'Dave' by his family and
friends rather than David, although this doesn't permeate
into his public life.

*"There is nothing to him. He is like a hollow Easter egg with no bag
of sweets inside"*
Charlie Brooker – satirist, critic and columnist.

FATHER OF THE HOUSE DAVIDS

The title given to the longest-serving Westminster MP:

David Lloyd George – Liberal MP for 55 years between 1890 and 1945
David Grenfell – Labour MP for 37 years from 1922 to 1959

BABY OF THE HOUSE DAVIDS

The title given to the youngest Westminster MP:

David Steel – Liberal MP for Roxburgh, Selkirk and Peebles at 26 in 1965
Dafydd Elis-Thomas – Plaid Cymru MP for Merioneth at 27 in 1974
David Alton – Liberal MP for Liverpool Edge Hill at 28 in 1979
David Lammy – Labour MP for Tottenham at 27 in 2000

MAGICAL DAVIDS

London-born **David Devant** (1868-1941) became one of the first 'personality' magicians. Rather than the dry and scientific approach to performing magic, which was the style at the time, Devant added wit and suaveness. He became an undisputed master of grand illusion and platform magic

– so much so that he was invited no less than three times to perform at the Royal Command Performance. Amongst his signature routines was the 'Magic Kettle', in which he produced, on demand, any alcoholic drink his audience called for.

Canadian sleight-of-hand expert **Dai Vernon** (1894-1992) was arguably one of the most influential card magicians of the 20th century. Nicknamed 'The Professor', he is alleged to have out-witted Harry Houdini when the great man insisted that Vernon keep repeating a card trick. After seven attempts to work it out, he gave up. Vernon would go on to use the title 'The Man Who Fooled Houdini' when advertising his shows.

Over the years **David Blaine** (b. 1973) has left audiences either astonished or sceptically non-plussed with his Houdini-like feats. Having made his name as a close-up street magician, he has proceeded to create a series of dangerous endurance stunts including being suspended 30 feet above the River Thames in a transparent box for 44 days without any solid food.

A minority of the British crowd reacted with mischievousness and a certain amount of hostility to the stunt. Eggs, sausages, a paint-filled balloon and golf balls were just some of the missiles aimed at the box. Blaine eventually emerged telling the crowd that he loved them all – and was immediately hospitalised.

"The last noted American to visit London stayed in a glass box dangling over the Thames. A few might have been happy to provide similar arrangements for me"
President George W. Bush referring to Blaine's stunt in a speech at Whitehall Palace, London

———◆———

FOUR OTHER DAVID BLAINE STUNTS

1. Being entombed underground in a plastic coffin box underneath a 3-ton water-filled tank for seven days, whilst surviving off nothing more than two to three tablespoons of water a day.

2. Being encased for nearly 64 hours in a block of ice with a tube supplying him with air and water.

3. Standing on top of a 90 feet high, by 22 inch wide, pillar for 35 hours, without a harness.

4. Holding his breath for 17 minutes and 4.4 seconds to set a new world record.

CONTROVERSIAL DAVID

German theologian **David Friedrich Strauss** (1808-1874) scandalised Christian Europe with his portrayal of the 'historical Jesus' in his publication *The Life of Jesus, Critically Examined*. In it he denied Jesus' divine nature and his theories revolutionised the study of the New Testament. On being elected to the chair of theology at the University of Zürich, the appointment provoked outrage and the authorities decided to pension him off before he began his duties.

"...the most pestilential book ever vomited out of the jaws of hell"
Lord Shaftesbury on The Life of Jesus, Critically Examined

SOME BAFTA AWARD WINNING DAVIDS

David Watkin (Best Cinematography): *Out of Africa* (1986)

David Leland (Best Original Screenplay): *Wish You Were Here* (1987)

David Hirschfelder (Best Film Music): *Strictly Ballroom* (1992) & *Elizabeth* (1998)

Geoffrey Rush (Best Actor): *Shine* (1996) as **David Helfgott**

JAZZY DAVE

In 1944, whilst serving as a rifleman in World War II, jazz
pianist **Dave Brubeck** (b. 1920) met saxophonist Paul
Desmond. Seven years later the Dave Brubeck Quartet was
born, with Desmond an integral part. It was in 1959 with
the release of the album Time Out that the Quartet went
platinum. With its offbeat time signatures, it included such
well-known tracks as Blue Rondo à la Turk, Pick Up Sticks,
and probably best known of all, the Desmond-penned Take
Five.

MEDIA PIONEERING DAVID

Belarusian-born **David Sarnoff** (1891-1971) pioneered
the idea of linking radio stations nationally over telephone
lines. He would go on to rule over one of the world's biggest
communications companies – the Radio Corporation of
America (RCA) – serving them in various capacities from
1919 until he retired in 1970.

Recognising the potential of television as a new medium,
he subsequently pushed through its development, which
led to the founding of the National Broadcasting Company
(NBC). In 1939, the first television show in America was
aired at the New York World's Fair, and was introduced by
Sarnoff himself. His nephew was scriptwriter Richard Baer,
who wrote for over fifty different TV shows including such
classics as *Bewitched* and *The Munsters*.

"Competition brings out the best in products and the worst in people"
David Sarnoff

⇒◆⇐

THEATRICAL DAVID

Actor, playwright, manager and producer **David Garrick** (1717-1779) was by far the most influential figure in English theatre during the 18th century. He developed and moved the art of acting away from a bombastic approach, to a more naturalistic style. There is a story that tells of Garrick being so engrossed in his own performance of *Richard III* that he was oblivious to a bone fracture in his leg. This is alleged to have inspired the theatrical felicitation of 'Break a leg!'

"His profession made him rich and he made his profession respectable"
Samuel Johnson

NOVELIST DAVID

Born shortly after his father was killed in action during
World War II, **David Morrell** (b. 1943) became best
known for his 1972 debut novel *First Blood*. Thirteen years
later this work became the starting point of the hugely
successful film franchise that starred Sylvester Stallone in
the role of John Rambo.

*"His name was Rambo, and he was just some nothing kid for all
anybody knew, standing by the pump of a gas station at the outskirts
of Madison, Kentucky"*
First line from the novel First Blood by **David Morrell**

———⟫•⟪———

A COUPLE OF STATESIDE COMEDY DAVIDS

When, in 1989, stand-up comedian and writer **Larry
David** (b. 1947) teamed up with Jerry Seinfeld, they
embarked on creating what would become one of the
most successful shows in American TV history. *Seinfeld*
would go on to run for over 170 episodes, although David
himself was not directly involved in the final two seasons.
He did, however, return to pen the series finale in 1998.
A year later he created the heavily improvised series *Curb
Your Enthusiasm*, in which he played a fictionalised version
of himself – a character that David claimed would be
exactly like him if he lacked any kind of social awareness
and sensitivity.

Born in Canada, **David Steinberg**'s (b. 1942) career aspirations shifted from the Church to comedy when he saw Lenny Bruce perform in Chicago. He went on to become one of America's best known comedians, and in 1972 starred in *The David Steinberg Show*, in which he played a semi-fictional version of himself as a talk show host.

This format would be repeated twenty years later when Garry Shandling developed *The Larry Sanders Show*. Steinberg has gone on to carve out a very successful career behind the camera, directing episodes of comedy shows including *Curb Your Enthusiasm*, *It's Garry Shandling's Show*, *Friends*, *Seinfeld*, *Newhart*, and *The Golden Girls*.

<hr />

CRIMINAL DAVIDS

Highway robber **David 'Robber' Lewis** (1790-1820) became known as the 'Robin Hood of Pennsylvania'. Predictably, many of the tales about him are more folklore than hard truth, but there exist newspaper accounts from the period, which tell of Lewis assisting the downtrodden.

Having escaped jail numerous times, he was finally apprehended and died from a gunshot wound received during his capture. On his deathbed, not only did he confess to all his crimes, but also told his captors about three large caches of gold hidden in Pennsylvanian caves. To this day, none of Lewis's stolen treasure has ever been recovered.

David 'Davie the Jew' Berman (1903-1957) was one of the pioneers of gambling in Las Vegas, and for a time 'looked after' the famous Flamingo Hotel following the assassination of crime boss Bugsy Siegel. Unusually for a gangster, Berman died from natural causes. However, his daughter, Susan, wrote a memoir about growing up in Mob royalty entitled *Easy Street*. In it she suggests that her father's death was mysterious and that her mother, an apparent suicide, was a victim of the Mob. Susan's own death – she was gunned down on Christmas Eve 2000 – is also shrouded in mystery.

Pharmacist **David Herold** (1842-1865) was a co-conspirator in the assassination of U.S. President Abraham Lincoln. On the same day that Lincoln was murdered, Herold's role was to organise the delivery of medicine to the home of U.S. Secretary of State William H. Seward, who had recently been injured in a carriage accident. The man to make the delivery was Seward's would-be assassin, Lewis Paine. The plan went wrong and Herold went on the run. He met up with chief conspirator and assassin of the President, John Wilkes Booth, but gave himself up when both were cornered by the militia. Booth was killed outright when he refused to lay down his arms, and Herold was put on trial. His only defence was that he was feeble-minded and Booth had been a powerful influence on him. He was found guilty and hanged alongside three other conspirators including Lewis Paine.

Arrested in 1977, **David Berkowitz** (b.1953), also known as 'Son of Sam', confessed to killing six people and wounding seven others in New York during 1976 and 1977. Berkowitz went on to claim that 'Sam' was his neighbour Sam Carr, who owned a Labrador retriever called Harvey. This dog was apparently possessed by ancient demons, and had commanded Berkowitz to carry out these killings. He was sentenced to six life sentences. A consequence of this case was the 'Son of Sam laws' which prevent criminals from profiting from their crimes, and that money earned from deals are passed onto victims or their families. The 1999 film *Summer of Sam*, directed by Spike Lee, is based on the Berkowitz case.

"There are other Sons out there – God help the world"
David Berkowitz

<hr>

FICTIONAL SPACE DAVE

Astronaut **Dr. Dave Bowman** first appeared as a central character in Arthur C. Clarke's sci-fi novel *2001: A Space Odyssey*, which then became a groundbreaking movie directed by Stanley Kubrick, and starring Keir Dullea. Bowman is sent on a mission to discover the source of an alien artefact found on the moon. But, he finds himself the only survivor following a malfunction in which the super-computer, the HAL 9000, takes over the ship

"Just what do you think you're doing, Dave?"
The HAL 9000 computer

NASA SPACE DAVIDS

David Scott (b. 1932) was commander of the 1971 Apollo 15 mission, becoming the seventh man to walk on the moon. But on his return, the mission became enveloped in scandal when it was discovered that the crew had taken 398 commemorative first day covers with them, of which a hundred had been sold to a German stamp dealer. Although perfectly legal – the money raised was meant for the establishment of trust funds for the crew's children – NASA decided to make an example of the crew, and none of them (Scott, Alfred Worden and James Irwin) ever flew in space again.

Scott went on to become a consultant on the movie *Apollo 13*, and the TV series *From the Earth to the Moon*. Of Scottish descent, he was briefly engaged to English journalist and popular TV newsreader Anna Ford.

Of Welsh descent, Canadian physician **Dafydd 'Dave' Rhys Williams** (b.1954) was a mission specialist on the 1998 Spacelab flight, and also took three space walks on a following mission in 2007. In the process he became the Canadian record-holder for spending most time on extravehicular activity – a total of over seventeen hours.

David Brown (1956-2003) was killed on his first space flight, when the Space Shuttle Columbia disintegrated on re-entry into the Earth's atmosphere. As a memorial, he had an asteroid named after him.

David Hilmers (b. 1950) flew on four Shuttle missions between 1985 and 1992, including the 1988 Discovery mission – the first flight following the 1986 Challenger accident where seven astronauts were killed.

David Walker (1944-2001) flew on four Shuttle missions, and was a technical consultant on *Deep Impact*, a 1998 blockbuster movie about a comet crashing in to the Earth.

David Wolf (b.1956) flew on four Shuttle missions and had an extended stay aboard the Mir space station. Whilst on board, he became the first American to vote from space in the 1997 Houston election.

⋙◆⋘

Some Olympic Gold Medal Winning Davids

David Hemery (GB)	400m hurdles
	Mexico 1968
Dave Schultz (USA)	Welterweight Freestyle Wrestling
	Los Angeles 1984
David Wilkie (GB)	200m breaststroke
	Montreal 1976
David Pelletier (Canada)	Pairs Figure Skating
	Salt Lake City 2002
Dave Wottle (USA)	800m
	Munich 1972
David Munson (USA)	Four Mile team event
	St Louis 1904

David Browning (USA) Springboard Diving
Helsinki 1952
David O'Connor (USA) Individual three-day event
Sydney 2000
David H. Bratton and
David A. Hesser (USA) Water Polo
St. Louis 1904

⋙◆⋘

MOVIE TITLE DAVE

The 1993 comedy ***Dave*** starred Kevin Kline as Dave Kovic
– an ordinary man who, as a sideline, impersonates the
President of the United States. But, when the philandering
President dies in potentially embarrassing circumstances
Kovic is asked by the secret service to 'fill in' for him.

He begins to enjoy his new role despite the presidential ambitions
of his corrupt and manipulative Chief of Staff. Written by Gary
Ross, *Dave* was nominated for a Best Screenplay Oscar.

FICTIONAL FARMING DAVID

In the BBC's long-running radio series, *The Archers*, **David Archer** (Timothy Bentinck) took over Brookfield Farm in 2001. Dependable and hard working, he is a valuable member of the Ambridge cricket team and is very proud of his cattle; and he is also rather fond of an old tractor that he has restored and named Rufus. David is husband to 'Geordie' Ruth, and father of three children.

———❖———

STRIPPING DAVID

Born in London and raised in Chicago, **David Rose** (1910-1990) was a twice Oscar nominated composer, a former husband of Judy Garland and an avid collector of steam engine boats and trains. Although he wrote award-winning themes for the TV series *Little House on the Prairie* and *Bonanza*, he will predominantly be remembered for his sleazy 1958 trombone-led composition, The Stripper.

Since then, this piece of music has featured in such films as *The Full Monty* and *Wallace & Gromit: The Curse of the Were-Rabbit* as well as numerous TV shows. But its most famous TV outing was in a much-loved *Morecambe & Wise Show* sketch involving the duo dancing to the tune whilst making their breakfast.

COMPOSING DAVID

In 1997 **David Arnold** (b. 1962) released Shaken &
Stirred, an album featuring new versions of Bond themes
and amongst the artists he used were Iggy Pop, Jarvis
Cocker and Chrissie Hynde. By this time Arnold was
already a Grammy-winning composer, having scored the
blockbuster *Independence Day* a year earlier.

An unabashed fan of Bond composer John Barry,
Arnold was in seventh heaven when he was asked to
take over the mantle for Pierce Brosnan's second outing
as the eponymous secret agent in *Tomorrow Never Dies*,
and has gone on to score each of the Bond films since.
He was also the composer for the BBC's hit sketch show
Little Britain that starred another Bond-aholic, David
Walliams.

⇨◆⇦

TRAGIC DAVEY MOORE BOXING DAVID

American featherweight **Davey Moore** (1933-1963) won
the world title in 1959 and successfully defended it five
times before losing at the Dodgers Stadium in Los Angeles
to Sugar Ramos in 1963. It was his last fight.

Moore collapsed soon after, went into a coma and died a
few hours later. Later that year Bob Dylan penned the song
Who Killed Davey Moore?

Like his namesake **Davey Moore** (1959-1988) held a
world title. In 1982 he became WBA Light-Middleweight
Champion and defended it three times before succumbing
to the experienced Roberto Durán just sixteen months later.
Like his namesake, he died tragically when his own car
crushed him against a garage door.

TV Sci Fi David

The holder of a Master's degree in English Literature
from Yale, the TV career of **David Duchovny** (b. 1960)
took-off in 1991 when he was cast as a cross-dressing
drug enforcement officer on the cult TV series *Twin Peaks*.
Two years later he landed the role of FBI Special Agent
and alien conspiracy theorist Fox 'Spooky' Mulder on *The
X-Files*.
Duchovny would star in the series for the next nine years.
Among other things, he made three appearances on *The
Larry Sanders Show*, in which, though he was playing himself,
he hilariously developed a strong sexual attraction for the
titular host.

"I'm half Jewish, half Scottish. It's hard for me to buy anything"
David Duchovny

INTREPID DAVIDS

David Douglas (1799-1834) was a Scottish botanist who, at the age of 25, went to the north-west of America on an epic plant hunting expedition. As a consequence he introduced over two hundred species of plants to Britain – mostly pines and firs – which were largely responsible for transforming the British landscape and timber industry.

He suffered a suspicious death a decade later. It would appear that, whilst in Hawaii, he fell into a pit set as a trap and his body was found alongside that of a bull. However, his injuries were not consistent with those of a bull's horns or hooves, and it came to light that the last man to see him alive was one Ned Gurney, an escaped convict who had set himself up as a bull hunter. There was a suspicion that Douglas may have been carrying some gold coins. Thus, the speculation was that Gurney had killed Douglas before throwing the body into the pit. Nothing was ever proved.

Having spent his early years working in a Lanarkshire cotton mill, **David Livingstone** (1813-1873) would go on to become Britain's most famous pioneering colonial explorer and missionary, enabling large areas of Africa to be opened up for trade and Christianity.

Having qualified as a doctor, he became a missionary in Central Africa. Livingstone was not only the first European to see Mosi-oa-Tunya (Victoria Falls), but also one of the first Westerners to make a transcontinental journey across Africa. And, although he would later wrongly identify the source of the River Nile, his observations enabled large regions of Central Africa to be mapped.

He firmly believed that his spiritual calling was more for exploration rather than mission work and as a consequence never forced the Christian message onto unwilling ears. On his final trip he lost contact with the outside world for six years before a journalist from *The New York Herald*, Henry Morton Stanley, famously discovered him living on the shores of Lake Tanganyika.

"Dr. Livingstone, I presume?"
Henry Morton Stanley

Itching for adventure, **David Pelham James** (1919-1986) left university in 1938 to sail around the world, and on his return he signed up with the Royal Naval Volunteer Reserve where he served as a lieutenant in command of Motor Gun Boats. In 1943 his boat was sunk and he was taken prisoner, but he escaped his captors twice – the second time successfully.

Following World War II he took part in a number of polar expeditions and, as a result, became an advisor on the 1948 film *Scott of the Antarctic* starring John Mills. It was with Robert Falcon-Scott's son, the naturalist Peter Scott, that he co-founded the Loch Ness Phenomena Investigation Bureau. However, this firm belief in the existence of a Loch Ness monster may have contributed to his downfall as Conservative MP when, in 1964, he lost his Brighton seat by only seven votes and it was speculated that his political opponents had used his stance on the 'wee beastie' against him.

ATHLETIC DAVIDS

One of Britain's finest long-distance runners of the 1970s was undoubtedly the moustachioed **David Bedford** (b. 1949). In 1973 he became the first and, to date, only British world record holder in the 10,000 metres by knocking over seven seconds off the existing record.

In 2003 he won a legal battle against a telephone company after they had blatantly portrayed a pair of British athletes in their advertising campaign wearing Bedford's distinctive red socks, moustache and shaggy hair, and then claimed that they didn't actually know who he was.

David Moorcroft (b. 1953) was a British middle-distance runner who, in 2009, still held both the British records for the 3,000 metres and 5,000 metres events. Although he competed in the Olympics, his only major medal was the 1,500 metres gold in the 1978 Commonwealth Games. Moorcroft remains the last non-African to set a world record at 5,000 metres.

PUGH

OLYMPIAN DAVIDS

David George Brownlow Cecil (1905-1981) – otherwise known as the 6th Marquess of Exeter, Lord Burghley or **David Burghley** – competed for Great Britain in three separate Olympics. Making his debut in the 1924 games in Paris, it was four years later in Amsterdam that he won gold in the 400 metres hurdles.

Elected to Parliament as a Conservative MP in 1931, he still competed in the 1932 Los Angeles Olympics where he won silver as part of the 4 x 400 metre relay team. It was Burghley who inspired the famous scene in the Oscar winning movie *Chariots of Fire* where Harold Abrahams sprints around the Great Court at Trinity College, Cambridge.

In the film Burghley was portrayed as Lord Andrew Lindsay and played by Nigel Havers. Burghley himself had refused to lend his name to the project, as the scene was historically inaccurate.

American-born weightlifter **David Berger** (1944-1972) represented Israel at the 1972 Munich Olympics. Having been eliminated in the early rounds of the competition, he tragically became one of eleven members of the Israeli team taken hostage and subsequently murdered by the Black September organisation – a Palestinian militant group.

High-jumper **David Albritton** (1913-1994) had a career that paralleled that of the great Jesse Owens. Both were born in Danville, Alabama; both attended high school in Ohio, as well as Ohio State University, and both were members of Alpha Phi Alpha – the first intercollegiate fraternity established for African Americans.

As well as this, both competed in the 1936 Berlin games. Albritton, and fellow high-jumper Cornelius Johnson, became the first black athletes to hold the world record in this event with jumps in the Olympic Trials. But, it was Johnson who took the gold in Berlin with Albritton taking silver. Predictably – as with their compatriot Owens – Adolf Hitler snubbed them when they came to collect their medals.

Having carried off a bronze medal in the 1,500 metres freestyle in the 2004 Athens games, Welsh long-distance swimmer **David Davies** (b. 1985) also entered the brand new Olympic event of the 10-kilometre open water race at Beijing in 2008. Having led for an hour and 40 minutes, he become virtually unconscious for the last 800 metres and had to settle for silver after an enthralling battle with Dutchman Maarten van der Weijden.

"I can't remember what happened, it was just a blur. My arms had gone, my legs had gone; it was just about what I had in the depths of my body."
David Davies

David H. Bratton (1869-1904) was an American water polo player who won a gold at the 1904 games in St Louis. Later that year he died of typhoid fever.

Also in the team was **David A. Hesser** (b. 1884). He died four years later. Both were members of the New York Athletic Club.

<hr />

MOVER-AND-SHAKER DAVID

One of the most influential figures in British television since its inception has been **David Frost** (b. 1939). A promising footballer in his youth – he turned down a contract with Nottingham Forest in order to go to university – he became secretary of the Cambridge Footlights just as the satire boom was taking off at the beginning of the 1960s.

This led to him fronting the groundbreaking satirical TV show *That Was The Week That Was*. In 1966 *The Frost Report* introduced viewers to the talents of John Cleese, Ronnie Barker and Ronnie Corbett. As well as being central to the set-up of two major TV franchises – LWT in 1967, and TV-am in 1982 – he has also presented the hugely popular quiz show *Through the Keyhole*. But, throughout his career, Frost has always shown a unique ability to seamlessly shift from relatively lightweight TV to heavyweight interviewing.

Interviewees over the years have included all the British Prime Ministers from Harold Wilson to Tony Blair and every American President from Richard Nixon to George W. Bush.

Indeed, the famous interview with Nixon became a film in 2009 with the part of Frost being played by Michael Sheen.

"Television enables you to be entertained in your home by people you wouldn't have in your home."
David Frost

———❖———

TV Dave

Dave is a cable and satellite comedy and entertainment channel available to British and Irish TV viewers. Launched in 2004 under the name of UKTV G2 +1, it was re-branded with the slightly less cumbersome name of UKTV G2.

Continuity announcers regularly mocked the length of its name stating that it had got '… more letters than Postman Pat'. It was re-branded once again in 2007 as Dave with the tagline 'The home of witty banter'.

"Everyone knows a bloke called Dave"
UKTV announce the re-branding of the channel.

———❖———

Some UK Single Chart-Topping Davids

David Whitfield: Answer Me and Cara Mia
David Bowie: Space Oddity, Ashes to Ashes, Under Pressure (with Queen), Let's Dance and Dancing in the Street (with Mick Jagger)

David Cassidy: How Can I Be Sure and Daydreamer
David Essex: Gonna Make You a Star and Hold Me Close
David Soul: Don't Give Up On Us and Silver Lady
David Baddiel: (with Frank Skinner & The Lightning Seeds) Three Lions and Three Lions '98
Craig David: Fill Me In and 7 Days
The Dave Clark Five: Glad All Over
Dave and Ansil Collins: Double Barrel
Dave Dee, Dozy, Beaky, Mick and Tich: The Legend Of Xanadu
Dave Edmunds' Rockpile: I Hear You Knocking
David Sneddon: Stop Living The Lie
Dave Stewart: (with Barbara Gaskin) It's My Party

TOP RATING STATESIDE DAVIDS

American screenwriter, director, and producer **David Chase** (b. 1945) contributed to such popular TV series as *The Rockford Files* and *Northern Exposure*. Then, inspired not only by his own upbringing, but also by one of his favourite films, *The Public Enemy* starring James Cagney, he created the multi-award winning series *The Sopranos*. The character of Tony Soprano's mother, Livia, was based on his own mother.

David Crane (b. 1957) is a writer and producer who is jointly responsible for creating, writing and producing some of America's most popular ensemble sitcoms of all time. The list includes *Friends* and its spin-off *Joey*, *The Class*, *Veronica's Closet* and *Dream On*.

Canadian-born **David Shore** (b. 1959) had worked as a writer on *Due South* before creating *House MD* starring Hugh Laurie, which became the biggest hit show of 2004-05 in the USA.

In 1982 **David S. Milch** (b. 1945) started his writing career in television by penning an episode of popular US police series *Hill Street Blues*. He would go on to create *NYPD Blue* (with Steven Bochco), and *Deadwood*, which starred Ian McShane.

David Sanford Kohan (b. 1964) co-created and produced *Will & Grace*.

<hr/>

A COUPLE OF BROADCASTING DAVIDS

David Coleman (b. 1926) is remembered as one of TV's most distinctive sports broadcasters and commentators. In his youth he was a successful amateur runner, winning the Manchester Mile in 1949. Five years later he made his first TV appearance on *Sportsview* – a midweek sports magazine programme.

Then, for a decade from 1958, he fronted the BBC's flagship sports programme, *Grandstand*. He also hosted *Sportsview*'s successor *Sportsnight* between 1967 and 1973. In fact, such was Coleman's drawing power that the programme was re-titled *Sportsnight With Coleman*. He covered every major sporting event both at home and abroad and during the 1972 Munich Olympics he broadcast for several hours during the siege that would result in the death of eleven Israeli athletes at the hands of Palestinian terrorists.

Coleman also spent eighteen years hosting the long-running BBC quiz *A Question Of Sport* and has been immortalised by satirical magazine *Private Eye*, where a column entitled 'Colemanballs' records gaffes and bloopers attributed to sporting figures.

"This evening is a very different evening from the morning that we had this morning"
David Coleman

The son of the first great on-screen correspondent Richard Dimbleby, and elder brother of fellow current affairs commentator Jonathan Dimbleby, **David Dimbleby** (b.1938) first appeared on TV in the early 1950s in *Passport* – the BBC's first holiday travel programme.

Early presenting roles included the popular 1960s school quiz *Top of the Form*, but it was in 1974 that he followed in his father's footsteps by taking the helm of the BBC's flagship current affairs programme *Panorama*. Twenty years later Dimbleby succeeded Peter Sissons as chairman of the topical debate programme *Question Time* which, in turn, had been inspired by BBC Radio 4's *Any Questions*, latterly to be chaired by his brother Jonathan. As well as covering major outside broadcasts, he has also presented every General Election Night results programme for the BBC since 1979.

"I'm in the middle of eating a Mars bar. Let's go to Sheffield Brightside while I swallow it"
David Dimbleby – caught on camera with his mouth full during the BBC coverage of the 1992 General Election.

CONSPIRACY THEORY DAVID

From a sporting background where he was a goalkeeper for both Hereford United and Coventry City, **David Icke** (b. 1952) became a TV presenter for the BBC when his playing career was cut short by arthritis. His career appeared to be going smoothly and a long broadcasting career beckoned.

However, in 1988 he became involved with the Green Party and swiftly rose to be their national media spokesman. Three years later he appeared on the popular BBC chat show *Wogan* wearing a turquoise tracksuit, and announced that he believed he was the '…son of a godhead'.

Despite public ridicule, he has developed his theories of the 'New Age conspiracy', in which the world is covertly run by 'The Illuminati', a powerful body of major political and cultural figures who, in reality, are reptilian extra-terrestrials. Amongst its number are George W. Bush, Bill Clinton, The Royal Family, actor Kris Kristofferson and deceased country and western star Boxcar Willie.

In a 2006 poll by *BBC Homes and Antiques* magazine, Icke was voted the world's third most eccentric celebrity. Ahead of him were singer Björk and ex-boxer Chris Eubank.

"I am a channel for the Christ spirit. The title was given to me very recently by the Godhead"
David Icke – announcement at his press conference in 1991

SPEED METAL DAVES

Full-on pioneer of thrash **Dave Mustaine** (b. 1961) was living off the proceeds of drug dealing until he discovered heavy metal and joined Metallica as lead guitarist in 1981. Alcohol and drug related problems followed him and he was sacked two years later. He then met bass player **Dave Ellefson** (b. 1964) and formed Megadeth.

Both have since become committed Christians even though Mustaine still maintains a reputation for feuds, grudges and slanging-matches with many other heavy metal musicians.

"I want to write something that makes it easy for young people to look right into the abyss" **Dave Mustaine** – on his music

CRITICAL DAVID

Dubbed the 'Rudest man in Britain', controversial media historian and academic **David Starkey** (b. 1945) has brought a vibrant take on his chosen subjects into the nation's living-rooms. When embarking on a career as a broadcaster, he soon gained a reputation for his ruthless interrogations and general abrasiveness on the BBC Radio 4 debating programme *The Moral Maze*.

Specialising in the Tudor period, he has made several related TV series, and more recently has chronicled the history of English kings and queens in the Channel 4 series *Monarchy*.

"Most (TV directors) labour under the creative delusions that they are auteurs. I think they've seen too many French films"
David Starkey

FICTIONAL COMEDY PALAEONTOLOGIST DAVID

In 1994 a new comedy show was piloted. The story told of how three couple's lives intertwined while sharing the same New York apartment building. Called *Couples*, it starred, amongst others, Helen Slater and Jonathan Silverman.

Another who auditioned for a role was Silverman's old school friend **David Schwimmer** (b. 1966). The producers of *Couples* decided to reinvent the show, and the result was the phenomenally successful *Friends*. Schwimmer was the first to be cast, as palaeontologist Dr. Ross Geller.

"It's a job – someone's gotta kiss Jennifer Aniston. The reality is, Jennifer and I can do our job well because we truly are friends. But when the day's over, she goes home to her boyfriend and I go home to a magazine"
David Schwimmer

'MORE FAMOUS THAN ME' DAVID

American concert promoter and TV producer **David Gest**
(b. 1953) spent a lot of the 1980s under the 'cosmetic knife'
and is famous for using the same plastic surgeon as Michael
Jackson. He married Liza Minnelli in 2002 with Jackson
as his best man, whilst Elizabeth Taylor acted as Minnelli's
maid-of-honour.

The marriage ended less than eighteen months later with
Gest claiming that she had been violent and physically
abusive to him. Minnelli, on the other hand, claimed that
Gest was simply after her money. In 2006 the British public
took him to their hearts when he finished fourth in the
popular TV series *I'm A Celebrity… Get Me Out Of Here!*

*"I knew I couldn't solve it. Because I couldn't figure out what made
her drink when things were going well"*
David Gest on his marriage to Liza Minnelli

⇒♦⇐

I'M A CELEBRITY… DAVIDS

Other Daves who have appeared on the UK's *I'm A
Celebrity… Get Me Out Of Here!* are antiques expert **David
Dickinson**, and former member of 1980s pop duo Dollar
and burger van proprietor **David Van Day** (b. 1956).

ANTIQUE DAVID

Born in Macclesfield but descended from an Armenian
silk trader, **David Dickinson** (b.1941) has become
as much famed for his catchphrases as he has for his
undoubted knowledge. 'Cheap as chips' and 'bobby
dazzler' can now be heard the length and breadth of
British car-boot sales.

He has freely admitted to serving time in prison for mail-
order fraud in his younger days, as well as dabbling in class
'A' drugs, but Dickinson became immersed in the antique
trade during the late 1970s when he was managing his
cabaret singer wife, Lorne Lesley. It was in 1998, and a
chance meeting with a producer which led to his TV career,
and it was two years later that the daytime BBC show
Bargain Hunt first thrust him into the public consciousness,
gaining him a cult status.

*"Tobacco perm-a-tanned with a proud badger bouffant... like a mutant
hybrid Arthur Daley and some check-clothed thing out of The Wind In
The Willows!"*
Loaded Magazine – Dickinson was number 72 in the
'Greatest Living Englishman'

⋙◆⋘

SATIRICAL SITCOM DAVE

Columnist and author **Dave Barry** (b. 1947) is one of
the few people who have been able to turn on their TV
and watch a sitcom partly based on his own life. For four

seasons, between 1993 and 1997, ***Dave's World*** focused on the semi-fictional ups and downs of Barry and his family.

The series, in which Harry Anderson played Barry, was based on his writings for the *Miami Herald*. In 1988 he won the Pulitzer Prize for 'his consistently effective use of humour as a device for presenting fresh insights into serious concerns'. His first novel, *Big Trouble*, was adapted into a movie and starred Tim Allen. However, its release was postponed in the wake of the September 11th 2001 attacks because the plot involving nuclear weapons being smuggled onto a plane.

"I can win an argument on any topic, against any opponent. People know this, and steer clear of me at parties. Often, as a sign of their great respect, they don't even invite me"
Dave Barry

GOLFING DAVIDS

Scotsman David 'Deacon' Brown (d. 1930) was, by trade, a roofing slater. He was also a keen and talented amateur golfer. In 1886 the British Open Championship was due to be played in Musselburgh and Brown was working locally.

Invited to play, primarily to make up the numbers, he astonished the professionals by winning the tournament. Soon after he turned professional, moved to the US and in 1903 was runner-up in the US Open Championship. Brown lost most of the wealth he had accrued in the Wall Street crash of 1929 and returned to Scotland where he died a year later.

Now a writer and broadcaster, Ulsterman **David Feherty** (b. 1958) enjoyed a successful career on the European Tour and PGA Tour. Less enjoyable has been his long battle with depression and alcoholism.

After having won the 1986 Scottish Open he woke up two days later at Gleneagles, forty-five miles away, and had no idea how he had got there. The trophy was lost and has not been seen since.

"Actually, some sort of exercise would have helped me. If I kicked the shit out of Tom Cruise, I'd feel a lot better about myself"
David Feherty, after actor and scientologist Tom Cruise had stated that therapy and drugs were useless, and that depression should be cured by physical exercise

⟫◆⟪

SOME OSCAR WINNING DAVIDS

David Lean (Best Director) *The Bridge on the River Kwai* (1957) and *Lawrence of Arabia* (1962)
David Niven (Best Actor) *Separate Tables* (1958)
David Bretherton (Best Film Editing) *Cabaret* (1972)
David S. Ward (Best Original Screenplay) *The Sting* (1973)
David Watkins (Best Cinematography) *Out of Africa* (1985)
David Brenner with Joe Hutshing (Best Film Editing) *Born on the Fourth of July* (1989)

David Shire with Norman Gimbel (Best Original Song)
Norma Rae (1979)
Geoffrey Rush (Best Actor) *Shine* (1996) as **David Helfgott**

<hr>

RADICAL DAVID

Pacifist and non-violent activist **David Dellinger**
(1915-2004) was one of 20th century America's most
influential radicals. Rejecting his wealthy background, he
walked out of Yale to live with down-and-outs during the
Depression.

During World War II he was imprisoned as a conscientious
objector and anti-war agitator, and took part in freedom
marches and protests against racial segregation. But, he
is best remembered as one of the 'Chicago Seven'. At
the height of the Vietnam War, Dellinger and a group
of protestors disrupted the 1968 Democratic National
Convention in the Windy City. They were arrested and
charged with conspiracy and crossing state lines with the
intention of inciting a riot. The subsequent court case
became a platform for putting the Vietnam War on a
very public trial. Although the seven were convicted, the
judgement was later overturned.

*"…There can be few people in the world who have crafted their lives
into something truly inspiring"*
Noam Chomsky on Dellinger

Astronomy David

German theologian and astronomer **David Fabricius**
(1564-1617) was killed after a goose thief, who he had
denounced from his pulpit, struck him with a shovel. But in
his lifetime, and with the assistance of his son Johannes, he
made two major discoveries.

The first, in 1596, was the confirmed sighting of a periodic
variable star – a star whose apparent brightness as seen
from Earth changes over time.

Having then turned their attention to the Sun, they
observed the movement of sunspots. This suggested that
the Sun rotated on its axis, and proved to be the first solid
evidence of this occurrence. Fabricius is mentioned in Jules
Verne's 1865 novel *From the Earth to the Moon*, in which he
fictionally claims to have seen lunar inhabitants through
his telescope. A crater on the Moon's southern hemisphere
bears his name.

<hr>

Ritualistic David

As a highly regarded Test cricket umpire **David Shepherd**
(b. 1940) became famous for his quirky ritual of lifting
one foot off the ground whenever the score reached 111
or multiples thereof. Known as 'Nelson', this figure is
considered unlucky for batsmen. One theory is that '111'
represents the three stumps without the bails, symbolising a
batsman being 'out'.

A Couple of 21st Century Sketch Show Davids

David Mitchell (b. 1974) met Robert Webb at Cambridge University where they were both part of the famous Cambridge Footlights. Together they would go on to star in the award-winning sitcom *Peep Show*, and sketch shows including *The Mitchell and Webb Situation*, *That Mitchell and Webb Sound* and *That Mitchell and Webb Look*. Mitchell has now become a mainstay of panel shows on both TV and radio.

"I've only ever bought one album for myself and it was 'But Seriously' by Phil Collins, and if there's a better reason never to buy another album then I'd like to hear it"
David Mitchell

Little Britain's **David Walliams** (b. 1971) and Matt Lucas met in 1990 whilst they were both attending the National Youth Theatre. But it wasn't until the mid-nineties that they actually worked together.

As a team, they first caught the attention in *Rock Profiles*, a series of spoof interviews conducted by Jamie Theakston in which Walliams and Lucas took on the roles of various pop and rock celebrities. However, it was with *Little Britain* that they would both become household names.

The versatile Walliams has also taken on non-comedic roles including a harrowing portrayal of comedian Frankie Howerd in the TV film *Rather You Than Me*. He is also a cross channel swimmer who, in 2006, successfully covered the 22 miles in ten and a half hours, and in the process raised over £1m for the charity Sports Relief.

"I was the kind of person who got bullied and loved the attention of it"
David Walliams on his school days

━━◆━━

ANOTHER NATIONAL TREASURE DAVID

Broadcaster and naturalist **David Attenborough** (b. 1926) joined the BBC in 1952 and has been with them, more or less, ever since. In 1954 he began *Zoo Quest* – a natural history programme which would take him all around the world. Over the next decade he expanded his experience by presenting anything from political and religious broadcasts to archaeological quizzes.

In 1965 he was made Controller of the new BBC Two. In his four-year tenure he gave the green light to such programmes as *Match of the Day, Monty Python, The Old Grey Whistle Test* and, with the advent of colour television, he brought snooker into the nation's living rooms with *Pot Black*.

Having served for a time as BBC TV Director of Programmes, and turning down the post of Director General, Attenborough returned to his first love of making programmes. It is estimated that a staggering 500 million people worldwide watched his 13-part series *Life on Earth*. He followed this up with the equally successful

The Living Planet and *The Trials of Life,* and this has been
followed by a whole series of 'Life' programmes. Amongst
the many comedians who have parodied him are Spike
Milligan, Marty Feldman, The Goodies and Michael Palin.

*"I don't run a car, have never run a car. I could say that this is because
I have this extremely tender environmentalist conscience, but the fact is
I hate driving"*
David Attenborough

A Homegrown 1970s Heartthrob David

From Irish 'travelling' stock, East End-born **David Cook**
(b.1947) had an early ambition to become a footballer and
was invited to join the West Ham United Juniors team. It was
as **David Essex** that he enjoyed a long and varied career.

At the age of 23 he was already lead actor in the stage
musical *Godspell* and two years later, in 1973, starred in
the film *That'll Be The Day*. The same year he penned and
released Rock On, which reached number three in the UK
charts, and led to a string of hit singles, and his tours were
accompanied by the obligatory fan-hysteria.

Diversifying further, in 1978 he played the lead character
of Che in the first West End production of the musical
Evita, and in 2006 he was lined up to play Jack Edwards
in the TV soap *EastEnders*, but pulled out due to other
commitments after the producers expanded the part. The
role went to Nicky Henson.

Publishing David

In 1905 Dundee-born **David Coupar Thomson** (1861-1954) founded D. C. Thomson Ltd and in 1936 the *Sunday Post* newspaper included a 'fun' section, which introduced iconic cartoon characters *Oor Wullie* and *The Broons*. Others were to follow including *The Dandy* (1937), *The Beano* (1938), *The Beezer* (1956), and legendary girls' magazine *Jackie* (1964).

A Couple of Liberal-ish Davids

David Steel (b. 1938) became one of the youngest party leaders in British history when, in 1976, he took over the Liberal Party at the age of just 38. These were evolving times in 'middle-ground' politics and five years later a group of disaffected Labour MPs formed the Social Democratic Party and teamed up with Steel's Liberals to form the SDP-Liberal Alliance.

After some early promise the 1983 Falklands War shifted public support in favour of Margaret Thatcher's incumbent Conservatives. **David Owen** then became leader of the SDP, and the often-troubled dual leadership of the 'Two Davids' began.

Savagely satirised by *Spitting Image,* Steel was portrayed as a squeaky voiced midget, who lived in David Owen's pocket. This, Steel believed, seriously damaged his image and undermined what the alliance were trying to achieve.

"Go back to your constituencies and prepare for government"
David Steel to the Liberal Assembly in 1981

David Owen (b. 1938) qualified as a doctor in 1962
and became a Labour MP four years later. He served
in various ministerial and shadow posts before, in 1976,
becoming Foreign Secretary following the sudden death
of his predecessor Anthony Crosland. At just 38-years-
old, he had become the youngest to hold this office
since Anthony Eden in 1935. In 1981, disaffected by the
appointment of Michael Foot as Labour leader, Owen,
along with three other moderate Labour politicians – Roy
Jenkins, Bill Rodgers and Shirley Williams – became 'The
Gang of Four' who formed and collectively led the Social
Democratic Party.

Having fought alongside the Liberal Party in both the 1983
and 1987 General Elections, **David Steel** suggested a full
merger of the parties. But Owen rejected this and what
would become known as the Liberal Democrat Party came
into existence. Owen remained to lead a shrinking SDP
Party, but eventually resigned.

*"...He's wasting his life now. It's so tragic. He's got real ability and it
ought to be used"*
Margaret Thatcher who stated that Owen's natural home
was with the Conservative Party.

CHILDREN'S TV DAVE

Stand-up comedian and actor **Dave Thompson** made headlines in 1997 when he was sacked from his role as Tinky-Winky in the children's TV series *Teletubbies*. He had allegedly suggested that the character he played might be homosexual. In response, *The Sun* newspaper started, and ultimately failed, in its campaign to get Thompson reinstated.

"… (Dave Thompson's) interpretation of the role was not acceptable"
The BBC

———◆———

FORBES RICH LIST DAVIDS 2008

31st	**David Thomson** (Media) $18.9bn
37th	**David Koch** (Chemicals, pipelines ranching etc.) $17bn
164th	**David Geffen** (Music, film and performance) $6bn
178th	**David** & Simon Reuben (Metal traders etc.) $5.5bn
214th	**David Murdock** (Food and real estate) $4.7bn
334th	**David Bonderman** (Texas Pacific Group) $3.3bn
358th	**David** & Frederick Barclay (Property and media) $3.1bn
428th	**David Gottesman** (Investments) $2.7bn
428th	**David Rockefeller Sr.** (Oil) $2.7bn
462nd	**David Filo** (Co-founder of Yahoo!) $2.5bn

DRAMATIC DAVIDS

Born in Scotland, **David Burn** (1799-1875) emigrated to Tasmania and wrote *The Bushrangers*, the first Australian drama to be performed on the stage. The subject of the play was the lives of convicts inside a penal colony, and the play was successfully performed in Edinburgh in 1829.

David Hare (b. 1947) has become one of British theatre's leading social commentators, often giving critical studies of deeply embedded national institutions such as the Church and the legal system. Plays include *Plenty*, *Pravda* which was co-written with Howard Brenton, *The Secret Rapture* and the trilogy of *Racing Demon*, *Murmuring Judges* and *The Absence of War*.

"...he (David Hare) is one of those writers who feels constantly obliged to take Britain's moral temperature through the chosen medium of drama"
Theatre critic Michael Billington

Another member of the politicised generation of theatre writers is **David Edgar** (b. 1948). As well as his 'State of the Nation' plays such as *Destiny* (1976) and *Maydays* (1983), he has also examined Europe – especially conflict in Eastern Europe. These plays include *The Shape of the Table* (1976), *Pentecost* (1995), and *The Prisoner's Dilemma* (2001).

He is probably best known for his epic two-part stage adaptation of Charles Dickens' *The Life and Adventures of Nicholas Nickleby* for the Royal Shakespeare Company in

1982. Subsequently adapted for the BBC, this was also seen as a morality play about England in the 1980s under the leadership of Margaret Thatcher.

David Mercer (1928-1980) wrote plays about the decline in British culture during the 1960s including *Morgan, A Suitable Case for Treatment* for which Vanessa Redgrave was nominated for an Oscar.

The son of a Yorkshire miner, **David Storey** (b. 1933) adapted his debut novel *This Sporting Life* into a film. Directed by Lindsay Anderson, both leading actors – Richard Harris and Rachel Roberts – were nominated for Oscars. Because the film budget would not stretch to hiring thousands of extras as spectators for rugby match scenes, Anderson deployed hundreds of wooden dummies to stand amongst the real extras.

Hard-hitting American playwright, screenwriter and director **David Mamet** (b. 1947) first gained recognition in the 1970s for his plays *The Duck Variations*, *Sexual Perversity in Chicago* and *American Buffalo,* and by 1988 was winning awards worldwide for *Speed-the-Plow* and *Glengarry Glen Ross.* As a screenwriter, he has received Oscar nominations for *The Verdict* (1982) and *Wag the Dog* (1997), as well as writing the screenplay for *The Untouchables* (1987). In the same year Mamet directed his first film, *House of Games,* which starred his then-wife, Lindsay Crouse, alongside long-time stage associate Joe Mantegna who would go on to voice mobster Fat Tony in *The Simpsons*.

"In my family, in the days prior to television, we liked to while away the evenings by making ourselves miserable, based solely on our ability to speak the language viciously. That's probably where my ability was honed"

David Mamet on how he learned to write violent, abusive and obscene dialogue

One of Australia's best-known stage and screenwriters is **David Williamson** (b. 1942). He has twice collaborated with director Peter Weir – on *Gallipoli* (1981), and a year later on *The Year of Living Dangerously*. Both starred Mel Gibson. His work as a playwright concentrates mainly on contemporary urbanised Australia. In 2002 he wrote the stage play *Up For Grabs*, which starred Madonna and ran in the West End for two months.

SOULFUL DAVIDS

Brother of Jimmy, **David Ruffin** (1941-1991) joined
The Temptations in 1964. Initially singing background
vocals, he took the lead when Smokey Robinson wrote a
song especially for him. My Girl became the group's first
number one hit. By 1967 his ego had grown along with his
profile and he was refusing to travel with his band mates,
preferring his own customised limousines. Also addicted to
cocaine, he was eventually sacked. Ruffin died as a result of
his addiction.

*"We are confronted with a problem that touches every one of us. We
are confronted with the most devastating slave owner of all times"*
Stevie Wonder at the funeral of David Ruffin

Dave Prater (1937-1988) and **Samuel David Moore** (b.
1935) together became **Sam & Dave**. Output included the
1967 hit Soul Man that enjoyed a second life after its use in
The Blues Brothers movie of 1979. Backing musicians for their
hits included Booker T. and the MGs, The Memphis Horns
and on piano Isaac Hayes who, in partnership with **Dave
Porter** (b. 1941), wrote most of their songs.

Prater died in a car crash and Moore went on to release
Dole Man in support of Republican Presidential candidate
Bob Dole in 1996, with the Soul Man lyrics rewritten. The
owners of the publishing rights pulled the plug.

Some Nobel Prizewinning Davids

David Lee (b. 1931) 1996: Physics
David Gross (b. 1941) 2004: Physics
David Baltimore (b. 1938) 1975: Biology
David Hubel (b.1926) 1981: Physiology or Medicine (won with Torsten Wiesel)
David Trimble (b. 1944) 1998: Peace (won with John Hume)

⟫◆⟪

A Couple of Child Star Davids

David W. Harper (b. 1961) played the role of Jim Bob Walton in the long-running American TV series, *The Waltons*. First seen in the 1971 film entitled *The Homecoming: A Christmas Story*, Harper subsequently appeared in the series for the next nine years.

Best known for his role as Jason Carter in the American TV series *Little House on the Prairie*, **David Friedman**, (b. 1973) retired from showbiz before the age of 13 and eventually became a marketing consultant. He also appeared in three special editions of *The Waltons*.

SAUCY DAVID

In the early 1960s American filmmaker **David F. Friedman** (b.1923), along with his business partner Herschell Gordon Lewis, made very low budget movies usually shot in locations such as nudist colonies. These were known as 'Nudie Cuties'.

Titles included *Nature's Playmates* and *Goldilocks and the Three Bares*. But in 1963 they made *Blood Feast*, a film that has often been considered the first 'gore' or 'splatter' movie. It also made them considerably more money than their previous efforts. Friedman would later move into the 'Roughie' genre, where the soft-core action was tinged with horror and a harder, more violent edge.

Output included *The Defilers*, *Scum of the Earth*, *Casting Couch* and *The Lustful Turk*. His career took a nosedive with the growing production of hardcore X-rated films, and although he was offered several directorial jobs, he declined.

"Sell the sizzle not the steak" **David F. Friedman**

⟫━◆━⟪

ACTIVIST DAVID

At the age of 34, **David Starr Jordan** (1851-1931) became President of Indiana University, the youngest university president in history. He was best known as a peace activist, where he argued that because war removed the strongest organisms from the gene pool, it was detrimental to the human species.

He was President of the World Peace Foundation from 1910 to 1914, and became President of the World Peace Conference in 1915. In 1925 Jordan was an expert defence witness in the so-called Scopes Monkey Trial, in which a teacher, John Scopes, was charged with teaching Darwinist evolution to his high-school pupils, instead of adhering to the Tennessee law which allowed only for Creationist teaching. Scopes was found guilty.

<hr>

PROBABLY THE TWO MOST INFLUENTIAL ROCK DAVIDS EVER

Born in Scotland, **David Byrne** (b. 1952) formed Talking Heads with drummer Chris Frantz, and they played their first gig as support to The Ramones at the legendary CBGBs in 1975.

"It's not music you would use to get a girl into bed. If anything, you're going to frighten her off"
David Byrne on the music of Talking Heads

The king of consistent re-invention **David Bowie** (b. 1947) released his first single, *Liza Jane*, under the name Davie Jones and the King Bees in 1964. But it wasn't until 1969 that he really caught the public imagination with Space Oddity – a hauntingly dramatic number that coincided with the Apollo moon landings.

"If I feel comfortable with what I'm doing, something's wrong."
David Bowie

TRUCKIN' DAVE

American country music singer **Dave Dudley** (1926-2003) was best known in the 1960s and 70s for his truck-driving anthems, including:

Six Days On The Road
Truck Drivin' Son-Of-a-Gun
Trucker's Prayer
Anything Leaving Town Today
Where's that Truck?
Dave Dudley, American Trucker

⟫◆⟪

ADVERTISING DAVID

'The Father of Advertising', **David Ogilvy** (1911-1999) began his career by selling Aga cooking stoves door-to-door. His employer then got him to write an instruction manual for his fellow salesmen entitled *The Theory and Practice of Selling the AGA Cooker*. This would become a seminal work in the science of advertising and selling for many years to come.

His simple principles included the notion that the function of advertising was to sell, and that successful advertising for any product was based on information about its consumer. Amongst many other achievements, Ogilvy would go on to introduce Schweppes to the USA, and make Dove the best-selling soap and skin cleanser in the world – a position it still holds today.

"Always hold your sales meetings in rooms too small for the audience, even if it means holding them in the WC. 'Standing room only' creates an atmosphere of success, as in theatres and restaurants, while a half-empty auditorium smells of failure"
David Ogilvy

<hr>

A COUPLE OF CARTOON DAVIDS

British author and illustrator **David McKee** (b. 1935) is one of the leading contemporary children's book creators, a number of which have gone on to enjoy TV success. His work includes *King Rollo*, *Elmer the Elephant* and, probably his most famous creation, the iconic *Mr. Benn*. Astonishingly, there were only thirteen episodes made.

"As if by magic, the shopkeeper appeared..."
Ray Brooks – Mr. Benn narrator

David Low (1891-1963) was a New Zealand-born political cartoonist who lived and worked in the UK. He is best known for the creation of the highly reactionary figure of *Colonel Blimp*, which savagely satirised the British conservative establishment of the 1930s and 1940s.

In 1937 he took a satirical swipe at Adolf Hitler and Benito Mussolini in his occasional cartoon *Hit and Muss*. With his work banned in both Germany and Italy, Nazi Propaganda Minister Joseph Goebbels claimed that this cartoon was highly damaging to Anglo-German relations. Following the end of World War II, it was revealed that his name had been found on a Nazi death list.

"It may well be, that the future historian, asked to point to the most characteristic expression of the English temper in the period between the two wars will reply without hesitation, 'Colonel Blimp'"
C. S. Lewis – Novelist and scholar

———◆———

GRUNGY DAVID

Heavily influenced by Led Zeppelin's John Bonham, **David Grohl** (b. 1969) became drummer with Seattle grunge-kings Nirvana. Following the death of Kurt Cobain in 1994, Grohl formed the Foo Fighters, primarily as a solo project but with the support of other musicians. He was also part of a band recruited to recreate the music of The Beatles' early years for the 1994 film *Backbeat*, and, continuing the 'Liverpool' theme, in 2008 he was a guest of Paul McCartney in a concert at Anfield football ground where he played guitar on Band On The Run, and drums on Back In The USSR.

"I was in awe of frontman Kurt Cobain's songs, and intimidated. I thought it was best that I keep my songs to myself"
David Grohl on secretly writing songs whilst on tour with Nirvana

DAVID BECKHAM TATTOOS

1. *Brooklyn* – his son's name on his back.
2. Guardian Angel on his back.
3. Victoria – his wife's name – but in Hindi – on his left arm.
4. Roman numeral *VII* on his right forearm.
5. *Perfectio In Spiritu*, meaning *Spiritual Perfection*, on his right arm.
6. *Ut Amem Et Foveam* meaning *So That I Love And Cherish*, on his left arm.
7. *Romeo* – his son's name on his back.
8. Classical art design on his right shoulder.
9. Winged cross on the back of his neck.
10. Angel with the motto *In The Face Of Adversity* on his right arm.
11. *Cruz* – his son's name on his back.
12. Second angel and clouds added to his right arm and shoulder.
13. Portrait of Victoria on his left forearm.
14. *Forever By Your Side* on his left forearm.
15. Chinese proverb *Death and life have determined appointments. Riches and honour depend on heaven* down his left torso.

COMPLICATED FAMILY DAVID

David Douglas, 12th Marquess of Queensberry (b. 1929) succeeded his father to the title in 1954. His eldest but illegitimate son has a half-sister who was married to Salem bin Laden – the half-brother and cousin of Osama bin Laden.

His half-sister has a daughter who was the first wife of gossip columnist Nigel Dempster. Douglas worked as Professor of Ceramics at the Royal College of Art between 1959 and 1983.

<hr>

SOME FICTIONAL COMEDY DAVIDS

Little Britain's **Daffyd Thomas**, (Matt Lucas) was a Bacardi and coke drinking, PVC wearing, attention seeking, self-proclaiming homosexual who lived in the Welsh mining village of Llanddewi Brefi. Having had absolutely no homosexual experience at all, he longed to be persecuted for his sexuality.

"Everyone knows that I am the only gay in the village."
Daffyd Thomas

In the BBC sitcom *The League of Gentlemen*, Dave or David was a recurring name. There was **David** – the bestial son of Royston Vasey's incestuous local shop proprietors Edward (Reece Shearsmith) and Tubbs (Steve Pemberton).

Then there was member of Legz Akimbo Theatre Company, **Dave Parkes** (Pemberton).

Finally, there was the frightening minstrel-faced proprietor of The Pandemonium Carnival, Papa Lazarou (Shearsmith) who sold pegs, collected wives and constantly enquired as to the whereabouts of '**Dave**'.

"You're my wife now, Dave"
Papa Lazarou

Written by Rob Grant and Doug Naylor, *Son Of Cliché* was a comedy sketch show broadcast in the 1980s on BBC Radio 4. Among its stars were Chris Barrie and Nick Wilton. A recurring sketch, with Wilton in the title role, was called *Dave Hollins – Space Cadet*. In 1988 this was re-invented as the cult BBC Two sci-fi comedy *Red Dwarf*, and Dave Hollins became **Dave Lister** – the dreadlocked, lazy, smelly, curry-loving hero – played by Craig Charles.

The Fast Show introduced us to **Indecisive Dave** (Paul Whitehouse), a character constantly in agreement with his mates in the pub, even though they always take opposite viewpoints, and he inevitably contradicts his own statements. Another character from the same show was cockney wide-boy **Dave Angel** (Simon Day) – an eco-warrior whose goal was to educate us on the state of 'good old muvver Earth'. Based on Mike *EastEnders* Reid, Angel's good intentions were frequently scuppered by his aging-bimbo wife Shirley (Maria McErlane).

Laboratory assistant **Dave** helped Professor Denzil
Dexter from the University of Southern California with
his experiments. This particular 'Dave' turned out to be a
monkey.

In a sharply observed parody of BBC Radio 1, Mike Smash
(Paul Whitehouse) and **Dave Nice** (Harry Enfield) were
two characters created for *Harry Enfield's Television Programme*.
'Smashie' and 'Nicey' worked as DJs for Radio Fab FM.
Both were based on a composite of a then-aging Radio 1
DJ line-up including elements of Alan Freeman, Dave Lee
Travis, Mike Smith, Mike Read and Tony Blackburn.

"In the words of Bachman Turner Overdrive, you ain't seen nothin' yet!"
Dave Nice

———◆———

DISC SPINNING DAVIDS

Having served his DJ apprenticeship with the legendary
Radio Caroline, **Dave Lee Travis** (b. 1945) joined BBC
Radio 1 in 1968. Over the next twenty-five years he covered
many time-slots and earned a number of nicknames on the
way. Originally he was just 'DLT' but, on account of his
beard, he became 'The Hairy Monster'.

This was adapted to 'The Hairy Cornflake' when, in 1978,
he took over the prestigious Breakfast Show slot from Noel
Edmonds. In 1993 the Controller of Radio 1, Matthew
Bannister, decided it was time to modernise the station

output, and the old-school DJs were culled. The most dramatic departure was that of Travis, who resigned 'live' on-air during his Sunday morning show.

"Changes are being made here which go against my principles and I just cannot agree with them..."
Dave Lee Travis resigns from BBC Radio 1 'live' on-air

Most recently a mainstay of BBC Radio 2, **David Jacobs** (b. 1926) was one of Britain's pioneering 'pop' broadcasters in the 1950s and 1960s, presenting the BBC pop-panel show *Juke Box Jury*, and then becoming one of the four original presenters of *Top of the Pops*.

Pre-Terry Wogan, he regularly provided the UK with commentary at the Eurovision Song Contests and away from the music industry, Jacobs spent over fifteen years as chairman of the BBC Radio 4 flagship topical debates programme *Any Questions?*

Although born in Hertfordshire, **Dave Cash** (b. 1942) developed a trans-Atlantic accent after spending time in Canada where he began his broadcasting career. However, in the 1960s he returned to England and teamed up with Kenny Everett on pirate station Radio London where they developed the hugely popular *Kenny & Cash Show*.

He went on to join Radio Luxembourg before becoming a pioneering Radio 1 DJ on its launch in 1967. Having joined Capital Radio in 1973, where he would spend the next two decades, he appeared as himself in the 1976 cult film *Quadrophenia*.

Another pioneer at the outset in 1967 of 'Wonderful' Radio 1 was **'Diddy' David Hamilton** (b. 1938). It was whilst making a guest appearance with Ken Dodd on *Doddy's Music Box* that he gained the nickname 'Diddy'. The name stuck.

Having cut his radio teeth some years before by hosting *The Beat Show*, Hamilton would go on to become a mainstay of the BBC network for over twenty years. Never shy of diversification, he also worked as a TV announcer as well as 'hosting' 1970s tours by such teeny-bop favourites as David Cassidy and The Bay City Rollers. Having broadcast on Radio 2 for six years from 1980, he eventually resigned claiming that the music policy had become 'geriatric'.

"There's only so much Max Bygraves and Vera Lynn you can play"
David Hamilton commenting on his resignation from BBC Radio 2

At the age of 18 Canadian-born DJ **David 'Kid' Jensen** (b. 1950) began his career on Radio Luxembourg, where his late night show concentrated mainly on 'prog-rock'. Indeed, amongst his fans was a teenage rocker named Tony Blair. Jensen moved onto Radio 1 in 1976 and became a regular presenter on *Top of the Pops* where he often co-presented with John Peel. Amongst the then unknown bands he championed were The Police, Tubeway Army and Frankie Goes to Hollywood.

VALIANT DAVIDS

Dave Gallaher (1873-1917) was captain of the first New Zealand national team to be known as the All Blacks. Although born in Ireland, his family emigrated when he was five and he grew up to play 36 times for his adopted country. He served in the Boer War and volunteered to fight in World War I where he saw action at Ypres, and was eventually killed during the Passchendaele offensive. Today, the Dave Gallaher Trophy is played between New Zealand and France, and is awarded to the winner of the first Test in any given year.

Born in Scotland but raised in New Zealand, **David Russell** (1911-1945) served as a lance corporal in the New Zealand Expeditionary Force during World War II. Taken prisoner in Egypt in 1942, he escaped from an Italian POW camp and worked alongside partisans assisting other POWs make their way back to the Allied lines. He was recaptured but refused to name his collaborators. Russell was executed by firing squad and was posthumously awarded the George Cross.

David Coke (1915-1941) was the son of the 4th Earl of Leicester of Holkham who became a flying ace with the RAF during World War II. Campaigns included the Battle of Britain and the Balkan and Syrian campaigns. Coke became great friends with fellow pilot and famed author Roald Dahl, and was awarded the Distinguished Flying Cross. He was killed in action over Libya in 1941.

A Couple of Palme d'Or Winning Davids

David Lean: *Brief Encounter* (1946)
David Lynch: *Wild at Heart* (1990)

———≡◆≡———

Legal David

American attorney and criminal defence specialist
David Kendall (b. 1944) advised U.S. President Bill
Clinton during the Monica Lewinsky sex scandal, and
then represented the beleaguered president during his
ensuing impeachment trial in 1998. Clinton was acquitted.
Kendall's career choice was heavily influenced by 1964
when he became active in voter-registration during
'Freedom Summer'.

This was a campaign in Mississippi to register as many
Afro-American voters as possible, because up to then they
had been almost totally excluded. At the time he was a
room-mate of civil rights worker Andrew Goodman who
was murdered during the summer by members of the Ku
Klux Klan.

ALMOST-A-CULT DAVID

In 1972 **David Cook** was the first presenter to star alongside Zippy, Bungle and George in the cult children's TV favourite *Rainbow*. However, following the second season he passed the role onto Geoffrey Hayes.

HIGHLY PHYSICAL DAVID

French-born **David Belle** (b. 1973) is the founder of Parkour: the discipline of moving from one point to another as efficiently and quickly as possible principally using just the capabilities of the human body.

An outstanding athlete, and coming from a family of skilled rescuers with the fire services, he laid the foundations for Parkour during his service with the military.

"...the physical aspect of Parkour is getting over all the obstacles in your path as you would in an emergency..."
David Belle

CHOCS AWAY DAVIDS

Actor **David Tomlinson** (1917-2000) excelled in what he
himself described as dim-witted upper-class twit roles and
starred in such Disney classics as *Mary Poppins* and *The Love
Bug*. In *Bedknobs and Broomsticks* he was cast as illusionist-
conman Professor Emelius Browne because, he claimed
to children, he was the only known actor who could sing
under water. A former flight lieutenant in the RAF, in
1956 he crashed a Tiger Moth near to his home. Charged
with reckless flying, he charmed the jury into a 'not guilty'
verdict.

Born in Kent on April Fools Day, laid-back cricketer **David
Gower** (b. 1957) played for England 117 times, scoring
18 centuries and over 8,000 runs in the process. However,
his record as captain of his country was less impressive,
winning only five times out of thirty-two, and on one
occasion he walked out of a post-match press conference
claiming he had tickets for the theatre. A man of very dry
wit and never above the odd practical joke, he once, on
the 1991 Ashes tour of Australia, flew a biplane over the
ground where his team-mates were playing a warm-up
friendly. Outraged, his captain, Graham Gooch, fined him
£1,000.

SOME TEST CRICKETING DAVIDS

David Gower (England): 117 Tests between 1978 & 1992
David Boon (Australia): 107 Tests between 1984 & 1996
Dave Nourse (South Africa): 45 Tests between 1902 & 1924
David Hookes (Australia): 44 Tests between 1977 & 1985
David Richardson (South Africa): 42 Tests between 1992 & 1998
David Allen (England): 39 Tests between 1960 & 1966
David Brown (England): 26 Tests between 1965 & 1969
David Holford (West Indies): 24 Tests between 1966 & 1977
Rev. David Sheppard (England): 22 Tests between 1950 & 1963
David Murray (West Indies): 19 Tests between 1978 & 1982

DANGEROUS DAVID

In 2003 paranoid schizophrenic **David Robinson**, a passenger on an Australian domestic flight between Melbourne and Launceston, became agitated and began to head towards the flight cabin. He was restrained by cabin staff and passengers, but in the process managed to stab a flight attendant and the flight purser. Both survived.

It was found that he was also carrying aerosol cans and lighters to use as flamethrowers. His plan had been to crash the plane into the Walls of Jerusalem National Park in

Tasmania, and thus release the Devil from his lair and bring about Armageddon.

WRESTLING DAVEY

British-born World Wrestling Federation fighter **Davey Boy Smith** (1962-2002) went under the ring name of 'The British Bulldog'. His middle name was the result of one of his parents mistaking the 'name' field on his birth certificate for the 'gender' field. Smith died after suffering a heart attack whilst on holiday. The autopsy revealed that anabolic steroid use might have contributed to his death, but no certain reason was found.

⋙◆⋘

INVENTIVE DAVIDS

David Alter (1807-1881) was the 'nearly man' of American invention. He trained as a physician, but because he didn't move around in the academic circles where his work would be recognised, he never attained the recognition due to him. Amongst his work was the construction of an electric telegraph that pre-dated the Morse Telegraph by a year, an electric buggy that was a forerunner of the automobile, an electric alarm clock, and a 'speaking telegraph' that pre-dated Alexander Graham Bell's telephone by a number of years.

Scottish-born **David Buick** (1854-1929) was two years old when his family emigrated to the USA. He would not only go on to develop a system for fixing enamel to cast-iron baths – the pre-cursor of the porcelain bathtub – he would also become the founder of the famed Buick Motor

Company. He had, however, no head for business and was more than happy for entrepreneur William C. Durant to take over as General Manager.

However, Durant's vision of a fast production line with minimal assembly costs was at odds with the craftsman Buick, who regarded each car as unique. Buick consequently quit his own company. He would go on to have a string of failed business ventures and died almost penniless.

"…I just got a few bad breaks. Anyway, money is useless, except to give one mental security"
David Buick

In the days of prohibition, **David Marshall 'Carbine' Williams** (1900-1975) ran an illegal distillery in North Carolina. During a raid in 1921, a deputy sheriff was shot and killed. Williams pleaded guilty to second-degree murder and was given a 20- to 30-year sentence. However, the prison superintendent noted his mechanical aptitude and granted him access to the prison's machine shop where Williams demonstrated his skill at fashioning replacement parts for firearms from pieces of scrap.

In 1931 he was released and set about perfecting his inventions. He soon gained contracts to modify firearms from the U.S. War Department. *Carbine Williams* became a movie in 1952 and starred James Stewart in the title role, with Williams acting as technical advisor.

FOLKY DAVE

In 1969 English folk musician **Dave Swarbrick** (b. 1941) joined the pioneering electric folk group Fairport Convention, and remained with them for fifteen years. In 1999 *The Daily Telegraph* was embarrassed into an apology after publishing a premature obituary for him. In fact, he had been admitted to hospital for a chest infection, but was very much alive.

"He read the obituary and didn't quarrel with any of the spellings or the facts – apart from the obvious one"
Jill Swarbrick – Dave's wife commenting on the obituary

———⟫◆⟪———

STATUESQUE DAVIDS

Donatello's bronze statue of **David** depicts the young king posing with his foot on the severed head of the giant Philistine warrior Goliath. Unveiled in the 1440s, it caused a minor sensation due to its portrayal of a nude young male.

"…a transvestite's and fetishist's dream of alluring ambiguity"
Mary McCarthy – American author and critic

Andrea del Verrochio's bronze statue of **David** was commissioned by the Medici family and installed in Palazzo Vecchio in 1476. It shows David triumphantly posing over the head of the slain Goliath. It has been claimed that the artist modelled the statue on the youthful Leonardo da Vinci who was, at the time, a pupil in Verrochio's workshop.

Residing in the Accademia Gallery in Florence, Michelangelo's **David** depicts the young, nude Israelite King David at the moment that he decides to battle with Goliath. Symbolising both strength and youthful beauty, it is arguably one of the most recognisable sculptures in the history of art.

Unveiled in 1504, it stands at 17ft in height and its apparently uncircumcised form – at odds with Judaic practice – would have been consistent with the conventions of Renaissance art. A copy of the statue at the Victoria and Albert Museum in London was given a detachable plaster fig leaf, which was added for modesty when visited by the likes of Queen Victoria.

Gian Lorenzo Bernini's **David** was commissioned to decorate the villa of Bernini's patron Cardinal Scipione Borghese in 1623 when the artist was still only 24 years old. It depicts David about to throw the stone that will bring down Goliath.

A-Little-Place-in-the-Hills David

Sixty miles north of Washington DC, **Camp David** is the 125-acre woodland retreat of the President of the United States. Quiet and isolated, it was originally built in the 1930s under the name Hi-Catoctin, and was initially used as a camp for federal government employees and their families.

In 1942 President Franklin D. Roosevelt renamed it 'Shangri-La', and had it converted to a presidential retreat. The name changed again when President Dwight D. Eisenhower re-christened it Camp David – naming it after his grandson Dwight David Eisenhower II. The complex of modernised wood cabins are said to be amongst the most secure facilities in the world, guarded by handpicked naval staff and US Marines. In 1978 it played host to the now famous Camp David Summit, in which President Jimmy Carter brokered a peace plan between Egypt and Israel.

———✦———

Presidential Davids

Born **David Dwight Eisenhower** (1890-1969), his family always called him by his middle name to avoid confusion in the Eisenhower household, as his father was a 'David' as well. Also known as 'Ike', he had a distinguished military career in which he became a five-star general and was Supreme Commander of the Allied Forces in Europe, responsible for planning and supervising the allied invasion of France and Germany towards the end of World War II.

In 1951, he became the first supreme commander of
NATO, but two years later, having retired from the military,
he successfully ran for President. Eisenhower's Republican
administration served two terms and swiftly fulfilled one of
his campaign promises which was to end the Korean War.
America enjoyed a sustained period of economic growth,
low inflation, low taxes, peace and prosperity under his
stewardship. However, in 1961, Eisenhower became the
first US President to be 'constitutionally forced' from office,
having served the maximum two terms allowed by the 1951
Amendment to the US Constitution.

*"Leadership is the art of getting someone else to do something you want
done because he wants to do it"*
Dwight D. Eisenhower

Up until season five of the TV series *24*, **David Palmer**
(Dennis Haysbert) was the President of the United States.
A prominent protagonist, only second to Jack Bauer
(Kiefer Sutherland), President Palmer was the victim of an
assassin's bullet. Because he was black, it has been claimed
that Dennis Haysbert's portrayal of Palmer may have
helped Barack Obama's presidential campaign. This is, of
course, unsubstantiated.

GRAND SLAM TENNIS DAVIDS

David Freeman (USA): US Doubles finalist 1943
David Pate (USA): Australian Doubles winner 1991 and US Doubles finalist 1991
David Wheaton (USA): US Doubles finalist 1990 and Australian Doubles finalist 1991
David Adams (South Africa): French Doubles finalist 1992, Australian Mixed Doubles winner 1999 and French Mixed Doubles winner 2000
David Prinosil (Czech): French Doubles finalist 1993 and Australian Doubles finalist 2001
David Nalbandian (Argentina): Wimbledon Singles finalist 2002
David Rikl (Czech): US Doubles finalist 2004

ALMOST SURFING USA DAVID

Guitarist and harmony vocalist **David Marks** (b. 1948) has been referred to as the 'forgotten' Beach Boy. Growing up across the road from the Wilson family in Hawthorne, California, he was not part of the original line-up when they recorded their first hit single, 'Surfin'.

However, when Al Jardine decided to return to his college studies in 1962, Marks was drafted in to replace him. Less than two years later, after a bust-up with Murray Wilson – father of Brian, Carl and Dennis – and also band manager, he parted company.

POPULATED DAVID

Built around its own cathedral, **St David's** (or Tyddewi) in Pembrokeshire, Wales is the smallest city in the UK with a population of under 2,000. It is also the birthplace of the principality's patron saint, Saint David.

―――――◆―――――

ENLIGHTENED RULING DAVID

One of the more popular monarchs was **David IV of Georgia** (1073-1125). Also known as **David the Builder**, he came to the throne in a bloodless coup aged 16 and proceeded to involve himself in all aspects of Georgian life. This included politics, education, the military and the active promotion of a Christian and more humane culture within his multi-ethnic kingdom. Today, the national flag is based on David's standard, and 'The Order of David the Builder' is one of the most prestigious decorations awarded by Georgia.

NEW MILLENNIUM HEARTTHROB DAVID

In 2000, English R & B singer/songwriter **Craig David** (b. 1981) became the youngest solo male artist to reach number one in the UK charts with his hit, Fill Me In. However, he is probably better known to a wider audience through TV sketch show *Bo' Selecta* in which he was portrayed as a bluff-yet-cool Yorkshireman.

Southampton-born David claimed that this portrayal had subsequently damaged his career, even though he willingly made an appearance in the series playing Craig Davis – a supposed tribute act to the Craig David character in the show.

A COUPLE OF 'RAZZIE' AWARD WINNING DAVIDS

Worst Supporting Actor of 1987 – **David Mendenhall** in *Over the Top*

Worst Picture of 1994 *Color of Night* – Buzz Feitshans/ **David Matalon** producers

---

ROCK 'N' ROLL DAVE

Influenced by the likes of Chuck Berry and Gene Vincent, Sheffield-born **Dave Berry** (b. 1941) was a teen idol in the 1960s. Dressed in black with collar turned up, amongst those who were influenced by him was one Bernard Jewry who would later become Alvin Stardust. Berry's best-known recording was the 1964 hit The Crying Game, which reached number five in the UK charts. However, this recording reached a much wider international audience in the 1992 Oscar-winning movie of the same name.

⬥

WHAT-A-WAY-TO-GO ROYAL DAVIDS

Dafydd ap Gruffydd (1238-1283) was Prince of Wales from 1282, but executed less than a year later. His supposed crime was that he had plotted to kill King Edward I of England. His death was not quick. He was dragged through the streets of Shrewsbury attached to a horse, then hanged. Still not dead, he was revived and then disembowelled and his entrails burned before him. His body was then cut into four quarters. He became the first prominent person in recorded history to have been hanged, drawn and quartered.

Ethiopian Emperor **David I** (d. 1413) was killed when he was kicked in the head by one of his horses. **David II** (d. 1540) was killed in battle and **David III** (d. 1721) died from being poisoned. His courtiers and a Muslim apothecary were found guilty and executed.

AND FINALLY - SOME DAVIDS THAT SHOULD HAVE BEEN INCLUDED...

David Brent *The Office* manager
David Strassman (b. 1957) American ventriloquist
Davina McCall (b. 1967) TV presenter
David Puttnam (b. 1941) British film producer and politician
David Hatch (1939-2007) Prominent BBC manager and executive
David Gulpilil (b. 1953) Indigenous Australian dancer and actor
Dave Gorman (b. 1971) Documentary-style comedian
Humphry Davy (1778-1829) Inventor of the Davy lamp
David Vine (1936-2009) Versatile sports broadcaster
David Koresh (1959-1993) Leader of a Branch Davidian religious sect
David Herbert (DH) Lawrence (1885-1930) English novelist
David Samuel (Sam) Peckinpah (1925-1984) American film director
David Sutch (1940-1999) Better known as Screaming Lord Sutch
David Davies (b. 1947) Singer and lead guitarist with The Kinks
Dave Hill (b. 1946) Guitarist with Slade
David Scarboro (1968-1988) The first Mark Fowler in *EastEnders*
David Yip (b. 1951) Titular actor in the BBC drama *The Chinese Detective*
Elizabeth David (1913-1992) British cookery writer
David Nixon (1919-1978) English magician and TV personality

David Threlfall (b. 1953) English actor and director
David Ackles (1937-1999) American singer-songwriter
David Filo (b.1966) co-founder of Yahoo!
David Broadfoot (1899-1953) George Cross-winning
Scottish seaman
David Hackworth (1930-2005) US Army colonel and
military journalist

...BUT THERE WASN'T ROOM

David Von Erich (1958-1984) American professional wrestler

David Lowe British composer of music for TV including BBC News themes

David Newman (b. 1954) American film composer and brother of Randy Newman

Dave Spikey (b. 1951) Comedian

David Hedison (b. 1927) American actor

David L. Anderson (1862-1918) American outlaw

David Suchet (b. 1946) English actor

David Brown (1913-1974) Australian rugby league player

David Edelstadt (1866-1892) Russian anarchist poet

David Henry Hwang (b. 1957) American playwright

David Parfitt (b. 1958) British film producer and actor

David Evans (1935-2008) 'Thatcherite' Conservative politician

David Lange (1942-2005) Former Prime Minister of New Zealand

David Myers (1971-2008) England and Great Britain rugby league player

David Mallet English music video director

David Powers (1912-1998) Special Assistant to US President John F. Kennedy

David Browning Trumpeter on the original *Coronation Street* theme recording

David Seymour (1831-1916) Irish-born soldier and police commissioner

David Healy (1929-1995) American actor and voice artist

David Miliband (b.1965) Labour politician

David Quantick (b. 1961) Comedy writer

David Davies (b. 1948) BBC correspondent and football administrator
David Thewlis (b.1963) English actor
David Diamond (1915-2005) American composer

There is every chance we have missed a David, or two.

Let us know at **www.stripepublishing.co.uk**

ACKNOWLEDGEMENTS

Thanks to Andy and Tony (aka 'The Raymond & Mr Timpkins Revue'), for lightly watering the initial seed for the 'Random Book of…' series. All at Stripe Publishing, and in particular Dan Tester for running with the idea. Jackie Alexander for proofreading, love, tolerance and support. Chelsea Blake for 'computer button-pressing assistance', and last but not least, all the Davids and Daves I know.

BIBLIOGRAPHY

The Hutchinson Dictionary of National Biography
Helion Publishing Ltd (1993)

The Tombstone Tourist Scott Stanton, Pocket Books (2003)

Sky Football Yearbooks Glenda Rollin & Jack Rollin, Headline

The Assassin's Cloak Irene & Alan Taylor, Canongate Books
(2003)

The Chronicle of the 20th Century Derrik Mercer, Longman
(1988)

The Chronicle of Britain
Henrietta Heald, Jacques Legrand SA International
Publishing (1992)

Fade To Black Paul Donnelley, Omnibus Press (2003)

Halliwell's Who's Who in the Movies
Leslie Halliwell & John Walker, HarperCollins
Entertainment (2003)

RECOMMENDED WEBSITES

imdb.com
nationmaster.com
nndb.com
sporting-heroes.net
behindthename.com
cockneyrhymingslang.co.uk
digitaldreamdoor.com
famousfolk.com
britannica.com
forbes.com
2spare.com
wisdomquotes.com
artistfacts.com
brainyquote.com
thinkexist.com
spacefacts.de
urbandictionary.com
chortle.co.uk
famouspeople.co.uk
didyouknow.org
thebiographychannel.co.uk
who2.com
cricinfo.com
biogs.com
grandprixstats.com
improbable.com
statistics.gov.uk
ssa.gov
Wikipedia